ORTHO'S All About

Vegetables

Written by Barbara Pleasant and Katie Lamar Smith

Meredith₀ Books
Des Moines, Iowa

Ortho® Books
An imprint of Meredith® Books

All About Vegetables
Editor: Marilyn K. Rogers
Contributing Technical Editor: Marcia Eames-Sheavly
Contributing Writer: Veronica Lorson Fowler
Art Director: Tom Wegner
Copy Chief: Catherine Hamrick
Copy and Production Editor: Terri Fredrickson
Contributing Copy Editors: Martin Miller, Jay Lamar,
    Chardelle Gibson Blaine, Diane Witosky
Contributing Proofreaders: Kathy Roth Eastman, Mary Pas,
    Jo Ellyn Witke
Contributing Illustrators: Mike Eagleton, Pam Wattenmaker
Contributing Map Illustrator: Jana Fothergill
Indexer: Dan Glassman
Electronic Production Coordinator: Paula Forest
Editorial and Design Assistants: Kathleen Stevens,
    Karen Schirm
Production Director: Douglas M. Johnston
Production Manager: Pam Kvitne
Assistant Prepress Manager: Marjorie J. Schenkelberg

**Additional Editorial Contributions from
Art Rep Services**
Director: Chip Nadeau
Designer: lk Design
Illustrator: Rick Hanson

Meredith® Books
Editor in Chief: James D. Blume
Design Director: Matt Strelecki
Managing Editor: Gregory H. Kayko
Executive Ortho Editor: Benjamin W. Allen

Director, Sales & Marketing, Retail: Michael A. Peterson
Director, Sales & Marketing, Special Markets:
    Rita McMullen
Director, Sales & Marketing, Home & Garden Center
    Channel: Ray Wolf
Director, Operations: George A. Susral

Vice President, General Manager: Jamie L. Martin

Meredith Publishing Group
President, Publishing Group: Christopher M. Little
Vice President, Consumer Marketing & Development:
    Hal Oringer

Meredith Corporation
Chairman and Chief Executive Officer: William T. Kerr
Chairman of the Executive Committee: E.T. Meredith III

Cover photograph: Walter Chandoha

All of us at Ortho® Books are dedicated to providing you
with the information and ideas you need to enhance your
home and garden. We welcome your comments and
suggestions about this book. Write to us at:
    Meredith Corporation
    Ortho Books
    1716 Locust St.
    Des Moines, IA 50309–3023

If you would like more information on other Ortho
products, call 800-225-2883 or visit us at www.ortho.com

Thanks to
Janet Anderson, Michelle George, Gina Hale, Colleen
    Johnson, Dave Kvitne, Aimee Reiman, Mary Irene
    Swartz, Margaret Smith

Photographers
(Photographers credited may retain copyright ©
    to the listed photographs.)
L= Left, R= Right, C= Center, B= Bottom, T= Top
William D. Adams: p. 24L, 38T, 61B, 67B, 76B, 89B
Cathy Wilkinson Barash: p. 29C, 34T, 37T,BR
Jack D. Butler: p. 10CB
David Cavagnaro: p. 8, 9T, 10L, 25, 26T,B, 27R, 28, 31,
    32CL,CR, 33, 35, 36, 38B, 39B, 41T, 43R, 44BL, 45T,
    46, 48, 49T, 51T, 53, 56T, 58BR, 59T, 60T, 62, 63, 65B,
    66T, 68BR, 69T,TR,BR, 71B, 75, 76T and inset, 80B,
    82L, 85B, 87TL,BR, 88T, 89T
Walter Chandoha: p. 12–13, 30, 47B, 54B, 72T
Rosalind Creasy: p. 21
Alan & Linda Detrick: p. 50B, 54T, 66BL; 86T, 87BL
Thomas E. Eltzroth: p. 19, 57B, 65TL, 67TL, 79RT, 86B
Derek Fell: p. 44BR, 52BR, 57T, 59C, 61TL, 73B, 74B, 77R
    and inset, 78
John Glover: p. 47T, 70T, 82R
George M. Henke: p. 72B
Jerry Howard/Positive Images: p. 6, 22, 23, 29T, 58BL, 84T
Bill Johnson: p. 65R
Dency Kane: p. 11B, 40B, 69BL, 83
Lynn Karlin: p. 24R, 64
Dwight R. Kuhn: p. 18C, 20, 26C, 32TL,TR, 40T, 49B,
    58T, 68BL
Michael Landis: p. 34 inset
Clive Nichols/Rupert Golby–Chelsea: p. 71T
Clive Nichols/Julie Toll–Chelsea: p. 7B
Maggie Oster: p. 39TR
Pamela K. Peirce: p. 45R, 76 inset
Diane A. Pratt Photo Design: p. 43TL, 81T
Susan A. Roth: p. 4 (Kristin Horne design), 7T, 37BL, 42B,
    79L
Richard Shiell: p. 34LB
The Studio Central: p. 9B, 68T
Michael S. Thompson: p. 10TC,R, 11T, 16T, 18T,B, 27B,
    32B, 41B, 42T, 50T, 55T, 66BR, 70BL, 74T, 80T, 84B,
    85T, 88B
Ron West: p. 39TL, 49R, 52L, 61TR, 73T, 81B

WAYS TO GARDEN SMARTER

Growing a garden should be an enjoyable hobby, not an endless stream of chores. Although you'll learn cost- and time-cutting strategies by trial and error and personal experience as you garden, the following tips and approaches will make any garden more rewarding and fun from the start.

Fill your garden with the vegetables you like best, but at the same time, set aside space for trying new things. Packed with lettuce, spinach, tomatoes, and squash, this garden reflects its owner's love of fresh salads—complete with bright, spicy nasturtium blossoms.

MAKE A PLAN

For many people, gardening provides an escape from date books and appointments. However, some organization in your gardening life is indispensable. By developing a good design, you can maintain a framework for a successful, fulfilling gardening experience.

Before you put that first seed in the ground, establish a plan. You can make the plan as specific or as general as you desire, though the more details you include, the more useful it will be. Although you can record it on anything from index cards to computer disks, the very best tools for a workable garden plan are simple ones—a notebook and a calendar. The calendar helps you to organize your schedule and keep track of daily tasks. The notebook allows you to organize your gardening dreams and to chart your progress.

Buy a spiral-bound or loose-leaf notebook that is divided into several (at least three) sections and has pockets on its cover pages or its sectional dividers.

In one section, sketch a garden diagram with measurements, row patterns, and a list of the crops that you intend to grow in each row. This arrangement may change year to year, so leave some blank pages for future gardens. The second section is for a planting schedule. The third section can be used for a crop diary, which is discussed in more detail later in this chapter.

Additional sections can be used for data, such as soil-test results, fertilizer and pesticide applications, and important phone numbers (your county agricultural agent's number, for example), or any other information you think may be helpful to have close at hand.

Use the pockets to store seed catalogs and other reference materials, receipts for gardening expenses, and photographs.

Remember: A gardening plan should guide you, not constrain you. Make any adjustments you think necessary to suit your changing needs or goals.

SPREAD OUT YOUR REWARDS

Although most people consider gardening a warm-weather hobby, you can grow vegetables from spring through fall by selecting crops that are adapted to specific seasons or by planting over a longer period.

In the dead of winter, study seed catalogs to determine which crops and varieties are the most suitable for your region. Concentrate first on those you can plant in late winter and early spring, such as carrots and snow peas.

Then consider what you'll plant in their place throughout the summer and into the fall.

If you're sowing high-yielding crops, such as those listed in the box below left, spread your planting dates over two to three weeks so the crops mature and bear fruit in succession, rather than all at once.

Or, if you garden in an area with a limited window of opportunity for planting, pick several varieties with different maturity dates. These can all be planted at the same time but will mature at different intervals.

Replant beds or rows when vegetables pass their prime. A small, intensively managed vegetable garden will be especially productive if filled throughout the growing season with a succession of different vegetables.

HIGH-YIELD VEGETABLES

Bush snap bean
Chinese cabbage
Cucumber
Leaf lettuce
Radish
Summer squash
Tomato

KEEP PLANTINGS SMALL

Bigger is not necessarily better in vegetable gardening. Large gardens increase your workload and may become unkempt if you can't keep up with them. They may yield more produce than you can use or give away. Small, well-kept gardens are more enjoyable and often yield better-quality produce. A 10-by-15-foot site is ample space for a diverse, high-yielding vegetable garden. However, even with limited access to land, you can garden successfully in pots and window boxes.

An easy way to determine the appropriate size for your garden is to estimate how many people you hope to feed from a garden spot. A 50-square-foot area easily can feed one person. Consider how much time you want to invest in working the garden and in processing and storing the produce it yields.

Think small when planting each crop. Try small plantings of a few different varieties within the same crop family. You can test new, unfamiliar varieties in this way without investing large amounts of time, money, and even emotion in a variety that may be a production or taste disappointment.

INTERPLANT

Interplanting crops saves space, looks beautiful, and really represents "outside the box" thinking. There are no hard-and-fast rules: Think of what will be going out of season when something else is coming in and which plants use similar space. For example, plant late-season leeks alongside beans. The beans will quit producing before the leeks are ready, and the leeks hold their own while the beans are growing. Quick-germinating radishes mark rows of slower-germinating carrots and are long gone when the carrots are ready. Plant lettuce between tomato seedlings; you will harvest it before the first tomato is ready, but while it grows, the lettuce controls weeds under the tomatoes and looks beautiful. Try garlic with eggplants, marigolds with melons, and cilantro with tomatillos. It's space-saving, weed-defying, and beautiful. Kitchen gardening at its best!

STAY ON THE MOVE

Vegetable crops are classified according to their botanical families (see the box below). Because closely related vegetables tend to attract the same pests and diseases and consume the same nutrients from the soil, too much family togetherness can cause problems.

To avoid these difficulties, don't plant related crops in the same spot season after season. For example, if tomatoes were in one row this year, move them to another location next year. Replace them with something unrelated, such as beans or watermelon. You should wait three to four years before returning vegetable relatives to the original row.

When practicing succession planting within a growing season, don't plant related vegetables, such as cabbage and broccoli, in the same spot in both spring and fall.

However, you can plant related vegetables in clusters. This will make keeping track of the yearly moves a little easier.

Follow crops, here mustard-family members broccoli and cauliflower, with vegetables from a different family next season.

PLANT FAMILIES

Apiaceae (Carrot family): carrot, celery

Asteraceae (Sunflower family): lettuce, chicory, endive

Brassicaceae (Mustard family): broccoli, cabbage, cauliflower, Chinese cabbage, collard, kale, mustard, radish, rutabaga, turnip, brussels sprouts, kohlrabi

Chenopodiaceae (Goosefoot family): beet, chard, spinach

Cucurbitaceae (Gourd family): cantaloupe, cucumber, pumpkin, squash, watermelon

Fabacae (Legume family): bean, pea, peanut

Liliaceae (Lily family): asparagus, chive, garlic, leek, onion, shallot

Poaceae (Grass family): corn

Solanaceae (Nightshade family): eggplant, pepper, potato, tomato

Keep plantings small: Stacked into a bed, chives, lettuce, parsley, and cabbage grow together beautifully.

USE MULCH

Mulch is an invaluable tool for gardeners. It takes only a little initial effort to apply, but the benefits are well worth it.

It can decrease your workload throughout the growing season and can increase yields by as much as 50 percent. Mulch helps control weeds, reduces erosion, retains moisture in the soil, modifies soil temperature, and discourages the loss of soil nutrients through the water table. Some types of mulch also add organic matter and nutrients to your soil.

A mulch is any material applied around your crop on top of the soil. Materials can be organic or inorganic. Organic mulches, such as sawdust, leaves, ground tree bark, partially rotted hay and straw or grass clippings, and even old newspapers, will break down during the growing season. These mulches can be tilled back into the soil at the end of the growing season. However, never apply organic materials such as sawdust or manure "fresh." Sawdust requires huge amounts of nitrogen as it decomposes, and robs it from the plants. Fresh manures burn plants.

Organic mulch layers should be about 3 inches deep around your crops. Because they settle and decompose as the season progresses, put down more than 3 inches initially. Apply fine-textured organic mulches, such as compost, about 4 inches deep. Bulkier materials such as straw, should be applied 6 inches deep. If you use newspaper, place them on each side of the row, three layers deep. As the mulches degrade, add some more material to maintain the ideal 3-inch depth.

Inorganic mulches, such as plastic sheeting (1.5 to 2 mils thick) or fabric weed barrier, cannot be incorporated into the soil at the end of the season, unless you use a biodegradable plastic mulch. However, many inorganic materials can be reused for several years.

Plastic mulches come in a variety of colors, including clear. Light-colored mulches and aluminum-coated mulches control weeds and help keep soil cool in the heat of the summer because they reflect sunlight. Clear mulches will not control weeds because the sun can shine through them, but they will help retain moisture and nutrients in the soil.

Black plastic mulches are commonly used because, besides controlling weeds, they

Mulched paths help to keep vegetables within easy reach in any type of weather. In this garden, a fine-textured mulch brings out the beauty of a patterned planting of leaf lettuce and red mustard.

Lawn clippings have all the characteristics of a good mulch: They suppress weeds, maintain soil moisture, help enrich soil with organic matter, and are free. However, they do tend to mat down and repel water. Mulching leafy greens helps keep soil from splashing into leaf crevices.

accelerate your planting season by absorbing sunlight and heating the soil, which may allow you to plant earlier in spring. However, as summer progresses these mulches can overheat the soil. Remedy this problem by applying light-colored organic mulches on top of the plastic as temperatures rise or removing the plastic when summer arrives.

PEST WATCH
SLUGS

Slugs are soft-bodied, gray, slimy, snail-like creatures that feed on plants at night, leaving numerous holes in the leaves and sometimes feeding on fruit. During the day, they usually hide from the sun in damp, dark places.

To control slugs, hand-pick them from plants at night or just before dawn. Or make a slug trap from a plastic yogurt carton. Bury the carton (without the lid) in the soil so its top is level with the soil surface, and fill it with beer. Place several of these around your garden and empty them every few days, restocking them with fresh beer. The slugs are drawn to the beer and fall into the cartons, where they drown.

Watering in the morning, rather than at night, also helps to discourage these pests.

WATER WISELY

Water is a necessity for a productive garden, but you should always water carefully to avoid creating extra work, added expense, and water-related crop problems. Proper timing, mulching, and awareness of your soil qualities can help avert problems.

For optimum production, vegetables need enough water to keep the soil around their roots moist, not drenched. If soil is saturated, there is no room for air, which helps plants take up nutrients and avoid root rot. Most vegetable plants need about 1 inch of water per week. However, larger plants, such as corn and squash, will likely need more water than smaller plants, such as peppers or salad greens.

It's rare for any garden to be successful without applying additional water (irrigating), especially during hot, dry weather. The type of soil in your garden will partially determine how much additional water is needed. Sandy soils or soils low in organic matter require more frequent irrigation than soils that are high in clay or organic matter. Clay-based soils can retain too much water, so beware of over-irrigating these soils. For any soil type, mulch will decrease your irrigation needs by holding water in the soil next to the roots.

When irrigating, try to saturate the soil to a depth of about 6 inches, then allow the soil to dry out partially before the next irrigation. Watering thoroughly once a week is better than watering a little every day. Too-frequent, superficial irrigation causes the roots to grow close to the soil surface, and shallow-rooted plants are much more susceptible to heat and drought stress than plants with deep roots.

If possible, irrigate early in the morning. Applying water to your garden in the late afternoon or early evening may leave excess moisture on and around your plants, which can promote disease and pest problems. And beware of watering when the sun is high. Droplets of water on the foliage magnify the sun and can literally burn your crop.

Most garden sprinklers supply about ¼ inch of water per hour. You will need to run the sprinkler for several hours to thoroughly wet soil.

If your plants are so large that their foliage intercepts the water before it reaches the soil, consider using a drip irrigation system. Typically, drip—or trickle—irrigation systems are hoses that are perforated with many small holes and capped at one end. These hoses lie directly on the ground beside the plants and are more efficient than sprinklers because they provide a slow (you'll have to run them for hours), steady supply of water directly to the soil around the plant roots. These systems often are more expensive than sprinklers, but they can save as much as 60 percent of the water that would be used by a sprinkler system. They are also safer if you must irrigate during sunny, hot times of day because they keep water off the foliage.

Soaker hoses are made from a porous material, which allows water to trickle out beside the entire row of plants.

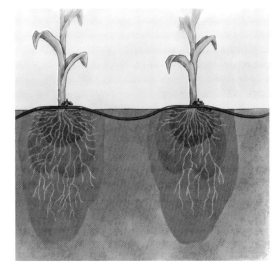

Strategically placed drip systems allow you to water the root zone of a plant and nothing else. There's no water wasted.

ANATOMY OF A DRIP SYSTEM
This type of drip system lets you put water only where it's needed. The system consists of heavy-duty black-plastic tubing and emitters, which you insert into the part of the hose lying next to a plant. Smaller spaghetti tubing lets you direct water to plants away from the main hose. A pressure regulator keeps the water flow slow and easy and a filter prevents dirt from clogging the emitters.

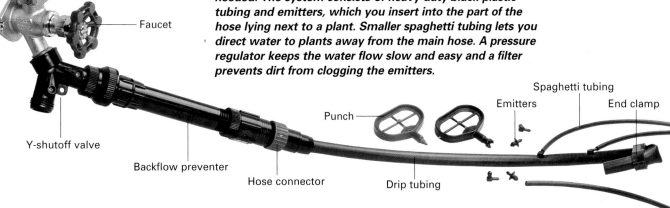

Faucet

Y-shutoff valve

Backflow preventer

Hose connector

Punch

Drip tubing

Emitters

Spaghetti tubing

End clamp

WEED EARLY AND OFTEN

Weeds cannot be eradicated, only controlled. Their seeds number in the tens of thousands and can be spread by wind, birds, insects, humans, and rain. Not only that, weed seeds can lie dormant in the ground for years before they ever rear their ugly heads.

Weeds compete with your vegetables for water, sun, and soil nutrients. If you leave them in the garden, they will reduce your harvest.

There are two types of weeds: annual and perennial. Annual weeds, such as spurge, chickweed and crabgrass, complete their life cycles in one year or less. They usually spread by seed. Perennial weeds, such as bindweed and bermudagrass, live two years or more and typically establish robust and extensive root systems from which they regrow each year.

The best weed control method is to attack early. Don't let them establish a foothold in the garden or give them a chance to form seed heads. Try to eliminate all weeds before they grow taller than ¼ inch.

Control methods include mulching, tilling, hoeing, hand-weeding, applying herbicides and solarizing soil before planting.

MULCHING: For most weeds, mulching is an easy and long-term cultural control. Mulch smothers weeds and also makes them easier to remove by hand if they do emerge.

TILLING: Rotary tillers are useful for controlling weeds along garden rows and walkways, but these machines cannot safely remove weeds close to the vegetable crop.

HOEING: In unmulched soil, hoeing is one of the best control measures. Not only does it kill weeds, but it also helps loosen any crust that may have formed on the soil surface. That crust can prevent water and fertilizer from entering the soil. When hoeing, work only the top 1 inch of soil. Working the soil deeper than 1 inch may damage the roots of your crop. Hoe lightly every few days. It takes just minutes to nip weeds in the bud.

HAND-WEEDING: Weeds located close to the base of a plant can be removed with a table fork, dandelion digger, or trowel. Insert the tool under the roots of the plant and lift up. However, you must take care that you don't also lift up the vegetable. For that reason, pulling weeds by hand is better in some situations.

Because weeds are easier to pull and you disturb less soil if the ground is moist, hand-weed after a rainfall or after you've irrigated the garden. Grasp the weed close to its roots so that you're pulling it out by the roots, not breaking it off at the soil surface.

After hoeing or pulling, you can leave annual weeds to wither and die and serve as a mulch for the garden. You can also till them into the soil for organic matter. Let the weeds

Field bindweed is a persistent perennial weed that spreads by seed. It is related to morning glories.

Quackgrass forms thick colonies. Any small bit of broken root will grow into new plants.

Bermudagrass, a perennial, spreads rapidly in warm weather. It easily invades gardens from below with its long wiry rhizomes, as well as from above, creeping in by stolons.

CHOICE TOOLS FOR WEEDING

Weeding tools include cultivator, fishtail weeder, knife, and hoe.

Weeding will be easier if you invest in high-quality tools. Start with a pair of rubber-coated gloves to protect your hands and get a better grip on weeds.

Fishtail weeders, also called dandelion forks, are indispensable for digging weeds. Slip the weeder under the crown of the weed, then lift up.

Use a hand cultivator to pry up clumps of grass. Slip the prongs under the clump and pull back on the handle like a lever.

Before buying a hoe, try out different models to see which feels most comfortable. Hoes come in various weights and handle lengths, so pick one to match your size and strength. Lightweight hoes with small sharp blades and long handles are best for routine weeding. Hand hoes and cape-cod weeders are great in raised beds.

A good way to keep tools in shape: Pour about a quart of used motor oil into a bucket of sand. Before putting your tools away, shove them deeply into the bucket several times. This helps prevent tools from rusting.

irrigate, apply fertilizer, or mulch a freshly weeded garden unless you have moved the pulled weeds from the garden or you're absolutely sure they are dead. These practices may revive your enemies. And don't leave weeds that have begun to set seed. There's bound to be at least one ripe seed.

You can toss weeds on the compost heap if the pile is heating sufficiently to kill seeds and roots. It must reach at least 140° F to do so. When in doubt, put weeds in the trash. Mowing around the garden before weeds form seed heads also helps prevent introducing weeds into your garden. Mow so the clippings blow away from the bed.

SOLARIZATION: The idea here is to trap heat under plastic and cook weed seeds, roots, and soil-borne pests, such as nematodes. In that way, you gain the upper hand when dealing with especially persistent problems and perennial weeds.

To solarize an area, lay black plastic on freshly tilled soil. Shovel soil over the edges to anchor the plastic and seal it tightly; leave it in place for six weeks. To be effective, the temperature of the soil 10 inches deep should rise at least 10°F. For that reason, solarization works best in sunny areas.

HERBICIDES: Apply herbicides with care to avoid damaging your crop or the environment. Most are formulated to kill specific types of plants—grasses versus broadleafs. To find an herbicide that will control the weed yet won't hurt your crop, read the label. If you can't identify the weeds in your garden, seek advice from local extension agents or knowledgeable garden center personnel.

Apply herbicides on still, windless days so that they don't blow onto neighboring plants. Always follow label directions, wear protective clothing, and store or dispose of unused chemicals carefully. A small amount of most herbicides goes a long way; use them correctly to save money and protect the environment.

FLOATING ROW COVERS FOR INSECT CONTROL

Many insect pests can be kept in check simply by placing a lightweight floating row cover over crops at planting time. These are made from a lightweight, spunbonded polyester that allows light and water to penetrate, but not insects. Use the lightest weight (about ³/₁₀ ounce) available. Heavier covers and ones made from plastic trap heat, which lets you plant early, when air is still chilly. Heat does not build up under the lightest cover, so you can leave it over plants all summer. If you use a heavier cover, you'll need to remove it when temperatures rise above 86°F; otherwise plants will scorch.

Row covers are highly effective if they're sealed so that pests can't enter. However, there are times when you'll need to remove the cover: when the flowers of insect-pollinated vegetables, such as tomatoes and melons, appear, when you weed (and weeds tend to proliferate under row covers), and, of course, when you harvest.

HARVEST PROMPTLY

Once vegetable plants have begun producing, harvest them frequently. This assures high-quality produce, because you pick it at its peak. Also, frequent harvest ensures continued productivity because after harvest, plants funnel energy into developing new leaves, flowers, and fruit.

Most vegetables reach their peak flavor and tenderness just before fully ripening. Seed packets often offer clues to look for to know when to harvest, but taste and experience are still the best gauges. When in doubt, it's better to harvest vegetables a little early than a little late. Also, produce harvested early in the day tends to be more flavorful and nutritious.

KEEP RECORDS

That handy notebook you started at the beginning of the growing season can help ensure future success and guard against failure. Use it as a diary of how the year progressed. In addition to reflections on your experience, keep records of the varieties planted, their performance, planting dates, yields, crop rotations, pest problems, and weather conditions.

Read your diary during those cold winter nights to remind you of the joys of gardening and to plan for the next season.

Pick vegetables in their prime to keep plants productive for a long time. Most vegetables are best when young and tender, but a taste test in the garden will help you be sure they are ripe.

Don't forget to take time to "stop and smell the vegetables." A shady seat at the garden edge is a fine spot for relaxation and reflection.

When selecting a site for your vegetable garden, it helps to map out your yard, noting any obstacles to good growth. You can make the map on a photograph of your yard, as here, or simply sketch it out on paper. If working from a photograph, be sure to shoot it from a vantage point that allows a view of the entire yard.

Morning shade

Shade and root competition from tree

Morning shade

Morning shade from house, replaced by afternoon shade from hill

Clothesline

MAKING A GARDEN

Gardens are more than food production sites. They reflect your personal style and taste and are limited only by your creativity and resources. To fulfill your gardening desires, a few fundamental requirements must be met. These include finding an appropriate site with good soil, sunshine, water, and air. This chapter will help you understand the basic needs of every vegetable garden and what must be done to ensure its productivity in your climate.

SELECTING A SITE

When choosing a site for your garden, there are many factors to consider, but think first of beauty and access. Is there a place in your yard that lends itself to the physical charms of a vegetable garden? Where will a vegetable garden look best in your current and future landscaping plans? Is that place easy to reach from your house, especially from your kitchen and the water spigot? Will you need fences or motion sensors and lighting to discourage vandals or the neighbors' dogs?

Next, consider what's already present in and around the area you select. A significant hazard for people starting new gardens is digging into buried utility wires or pipes. Rupturing or cutting one of these lines can cause utility outages and can be dangerous. If you're unsure about the location of underground lines in your yard, call your local utility companies. They will send personnel out to mark the lines' paths for you.

Also, keep in mind that almost all gardens need irrigation. So choose a spot that is close to an accessible source of water or install a water line to make irrigation easier on you.

GROWING CONDITIONS: Of course, the most important consideration when selecting a site for your vegetable garden is ensuring that it meets plant requirements.

SUNLIGHT: Look for a spot away from shrubs and trees. Their root systems will compete

Slope

SELECTING A SITE
continued

with crops for moisture and nutrients, and they may shade them. All vegetables need eight hours or more of direct sunlight. The surest way to select a site with that much sun is to observe the sun and shade patterns in your yard throughout a summer day. A little shade cast by buildings or trees will not hurt your crop, and in hotter regions, intermittent, late-afternoon shade may be helpful. But if shade is cast on your site for more than two hours a day, pick another spot or plan to grow only shade-tolerant crops, such as salad greens, beets, and cabbages.

AIR CIRCULATION: Moderate air circulation reduces the possibility and severity of disease because breezes help to dry foliage. Damp, still environments promote the spread of fungal and bacterial diseases. Pick a site where air can flow. If you live where strong prevailing winds are common, windbreaks may protect your crops from severe gusts.

LOW SPOTS: Low-lying areas or areas shielded by shrubs, trees, or fences may thwart good air circulation and can also become "frost pockets." Cold air naturally drains into low areas and so frost can settle on your crop even when surrounding areas are frost free. If you plant in a frost pocket, your growing season is likely to be shorter and the risk of freeze damage higher.

WATER DRAINAGE: Few crops thrive if their "feet" are always wet. They can't absorb nutrients, and roots may rot. Pick a site that isn't prone to floods or standing water. If your only site tends to be wet, some problems can be overcome by cultivation, raised beds, or drainage systems.

Sometimes drainage is a problem because the subsoil (the layer of soil below your topsoil) has become compacted and formed a "hardpan," an impermeable layer of soil. Tilling deeply before you plant a garden can help shatter this pan and improve drainage.

If a complex drainage system is required, it's best to consult a specialist, such as a soil engineer or landscape architect. For small problems, you can try some simple drainage systems, such as installing trenches and perforated plastic drainage pipes. The trenches should be 18 inches deep and about 4 feet apart. Lay the pipes in these trenches and cover them with 1 inch of gravel, then fill the remaining portion of the trench to ground level with topsoil. Arrange trenches so they direct water away from the garden. Take care not to direct the flow where it may create yet another wet spot in your yard.

Raised beds are another option in poorly drained areas: Mound topsoil to form a seed bed at least 4 inches higher than ground level. If you are building beds to manage drainage problems, leave trenches in between the beds so water can exit the site.

ROWS, RAISED BEDS, AND CONTAINERS

Garden arrangement is a matter of personal taste, convenience, and available space. Traditionally, people have planted vegetables in rows, which are easier to cultivate, manage sunlight, and harvest than meandering rows. However, that shouldn't prevent you from creating a unique pattern in your garden if that's what you want. There are just a few guidelines to follow to ensure whatever pattern you create is productive.

Plant tall crops, such as corn and okra, on the north side of the garden to keep them from overshading smaller crops, or on the south side if you want to cast intermittent shade on smaller, heat-sensitive crops.

Spacing varies greatly depending on what you are planting and as much as possible, you should follow the recommended spacing for the best productivity. Seed packets usually provide specific spacing information. But, in general, rambling crops, such as squash and watermelon, need 4- to 6-foot-wide rows with plants spaced 2 to 3 feet apart within the row. Large plants, such as okra and eggplant, need rows at least 3 feet wide and should be spaced 30 inches apart in the row. Smaller plants, such as onions and radishes, can tolerate rows 8 to 9 inches wide and can be planted 2 to 4 inches apart.

In gardens that you intend to hand-cultivate, you can sow seed closer than these guidelines because you don't have to take equipment into the plot. Plant crops close enough for them to develop a closed canopy over the soil as they mature. The canopy keeps soil under the plants moist and cool and shades out weeds.

RAISED BEDS: Raised beds provide several advantages. They eliminate drainage problems and require less bending and stooping. Often,

SHADE-TOLERANT VEGETABLES

No vegetable plants will grow in heavy shade, but many leafy greens can get by with only four to six hours of direct sunlight. As long as they have adequate spacing, the following vegetables are good candidates to grow in partial shade: arugula, chard, collards, leaf lettuce, spinach, and kale.

yields are higher because you have more control over soil quality. The design of a raised bed should suit your needs. Some people simply contour their soil into high rows, while others construct a frame to form beds.

Frames can be made of wood, brick, concrete blocks, or plastic boards. Use cedar, redwood, or landscape timbers for wooden frames. Avoid creosote or chemically treated lumber because they may leach chemicals, and contaminate both the soil and your food.

An ideal size for a raised bed is 4 feet wide. At this width, you can easily reach into the center of the bed from either side. Length will depend on available space and personal preference. However, extremely long raised beds can be harder to manage than short beds.

Orient raised beds on a north-south basis if you're planting low-growing crops, and on an east-west axis if you are growing taller crops.

Before building a raised bed, till or loosen the base soil. Then add good-quality top soil and additional organic matter. Test the soil, then fertilize it based on the results. In a raised bed, you literally create your own soil, so make the best possible.

CONTAINERS: Window-box and container gardens are quite popular for people who live in cities or have limited access to land. They do limit the crops you can grow. Smaller vegetables, such as tomatoes and peppers, work beautifully. To gain more space, think up. Train vines such as cucumbers on trellises. Stake tomatoes. Put pole beans on tepees.

Because every inch can be used for crops, raised beds make efficient use of space, like this salad-green-filled garden.

ROOM TO MOVE

As you lay out your garden, consider not only the space your plants will need. You'll want to have ample space to weed and harvest. How much space between rows that will require depends mostly on the size and design of your garden and the equipment you plan to use.

If the garden is small enough to reach all parts from the side, you need not leave room to move within the garden. But if your garden is so large that you have to get into it to weed or harvest, add walkways. A foot or two between rows is plenty of room to bend and squat. Add more space if you plan to use a garden cart between rows. To determine how much more room, measure your vehicle and add 2 inches to each side. If you plan to mow between rows to control grass and weeds, measure the mower and add 4 inches. For long rows, you may need wider middles to turn your equipment.

'Ruby Ball' cabbage and 'Bibb' lettuce make fine pot partners. The lettuce will be ready to harvest by the time the cabbage spreads to fill the space.

VEGETABLES IN CONTAINERS

Most vegetables grow quite well in containers such as pots, boxes, tubs, gallon cans, or even bushel baskets. Large, broad containers are ideal because they retain more moisture than small, narrow pots. Pots 6 to 10 inches in diameter are fine for small crops, such as many herbs and green onions. For larger vegetables, such as tomatoes, peppers, and eggplant, 5-gallon containers are a better choice.

Container-grown vegetables require more frequent watering and fertilizing than in-ground plants because they're limited only to what is available in the pot. Make sure your containers have holes in the bottom for drainage and use a high-quality potting soil. Do not use garden soil.

Crops suited for container growing include cherry tomatoes, small-fruited peppers, bush beans, small carrots, salad greens, and dwarf cucumbers and squash.

START WITH THE SOIL

Basic digging tools include a shovel and square spade for preparing beds and planting holes and for incorporating amendments. Harvest root crops with a digging fork. Use a hand trowel to tuck in small seedlings.

Vegetables thrive and taste better if they grow in good soil. A high-quality soil is one that is fertile (soil that contains enough nutrients to support the plants) and has a physical structure that provides the proper balance of air and water around the roots.

Soil itself is composed of a mixture of mineral particles, organic matter, air, and water. Desirable soils should be about 45 percent mineral, 5 percent organic matter, 25 percent air, and 25 percent water.

Two layers of soil are important to a home garden—topsoil, which is the layer of soil closest to the surface, and subsoil, which is the layer immediately below the topsoil.

Topsoil is where most plant roots reside, and it's the place plants need the most organic matter and fertility. Ideally, the topsoil layer should be at least 18 to 20 inches deep. It should be porous enough for air and water to move through. A soil test can provide you with information on the quality of your topsoil, its structure and fertility, plus advise you on any amendments you may need to add to improve its condition.

In many sites, erosion has diminished the amount of topsoil available for planting. If your topsoil is shallow, consider buying a load and spreading it on your garden area. Buy enough to cover the entire area 4 to 6 inches deep. Before buying, check the soil to ensure that it is of high quality.

Subsoil tends to be more compact and denser than topsoil. If it's too compacted, it will restrict water flow and root growth. In many places, the subsoil has become so compacted it has formed a hardpan. If you encounter a hardpan within 18 inches of the soil surface, break it up by double digging.

CLAY, SAND, AND LOAM

The texture of soil is determined by the type and size of mineral particles it contains. These particles are divided into three categories: sand, silt, and clay. Clay has the smallest particles and sand the largest.

The most desirable soil—loam—has a mixture of all three particle types. A loamy soil is soft textured and rich in organic matter. It is easy to work, yet holds moisture well.

Usually soils have an excess of one particle type or another, which can cause problems. Too much clay forms hard clods and makes the soil clump together and difficult to

Tiny mineral particles make up clay soil (left), which prevents air and water movement. Water puddles on top. Sand's large particles let water pass right through (center). Loam (right) has the best mix of large and small particles. It holds moisture yet leaves room for air.

Roots and tubers develop best in high-quality topsoil that is fertile and has a good structure, which allows water and air to move freely.

cultivate. When wet, it's sticky and impossible to work. Because clay soils are not porous, little air and water moves through them. Too much sand in soil makes for a loose soil texture, and while this makes it easy to work, it will not retain water or nutrients.

SOIL AMENDMENTS

If you aren't blessed with perfect soil, fear not. You always can improve soil quality by adding organic matter, such as compost and manure.

Organic matter comes in many forms, from commercially produced materials to free waste products. Any soil will benefit from added organic matter. Organic matter is formed by decomposing animal or plant material. It is rich in nutrients and helps maintain good soil texture. It provides a favorable environment for microorganisms that help decompose additional organic material and release nutrients. Soils rich in organic matter tend to be dark brown or black in color.

Sources of organic matter include decayed leaves, sawdust, or grasses (including lawn clippings, straw, and hay), peat moss, ground tree bark, compost, and animal manure. Avoid sources of organic matter that may have been contaminated with weed seeds or pesticide residue.

As you add organic matter, work it into the upper 3 to 6 inches of soil. You may not have to add significant amounts every year, but it certainly won't hurt to add a little every time you dig in the garden.

COMPOST: Compost is decomposed organic matter. You can make your own from the steady supply of organic material found in your home and yard, from kitchen scraps to yard waste. Appropriate items for composting are kitchen scraps, garden waste, lawn clippings, sawdust, and manure. Avoid meats or heavily oiled items; these draw unwelcome animals, such as rodents, into your yard and can actually slow down the composting process. Larger items, such as tree branches, should be chopped or shredded before putting them on the compost pile so they take up less room and break down more rapidly. Unless you can guarantee that your compost piles heats to 140° F, don't throw weeds or diseased plants onto the pile; otherwise you risk spreading these problems.

A compost pile can be merely a heap in the back corner of your yard, or a more formal structure, such as a wood or wire-mesh container, or even a commercially made bin. An ideal size for a compost pile is 4 cubic feet (4 feet tall, wide, and long).

Put the pile in a shady, well-drained area. If starting it on open ground, till or dig the soil underneath before you begin to fill the area.

TEST YOUR SOIL!

To truly know your soil, test it. Results of the test will provide guidelines on how much lime and fertilizer to add to your garden.

You should test soil annually because your soil changes as you plant, add organic matter, and fertilize the garden. In most states, soil test kits and instructions are available from local extension offices and from private laboratories. Testing fees are affordable and the results are well worth the expense.

You might also consider using one of the do-it-yourself kits available at nurseries and garden centers. Soil test results from the do-it-yourself kits will tell you how much fertilizer to add to the soil, but they will not supply you with exact application rates and timing. For this information, take the test results to your local extension agent or to a fertilizer supplier.

If possible, sample the soil in late fall or early winter. In that way, if results indicate you need to apply lime to the soil, it will have enough time to work to balance soil pH. You will also be assured of "beating the crowds" when sending the soil sample to a lab or extension office for analysis.

TEST FOR TEXTURE:
Checking whether your soil is sand, clay, or loam is simple. You can do it at home. Place about a quarter cup of soil into a pint jar. Fill the jar with water, put the lid on, then shake it up. Set the jar in an out-of-way spot for a few days and wait for the various components of the soil to form layers as they settle out.

Sand settles to the bottom of the jar first. It's the heaviest particle in soil. The next layer will be silt. Over that, you'll find organic matter. The top layer is clay, the finest and lightest weight component of soil. In fact, it is so lightweight, it may take weeks to settle and you'll recognize it only by the cloudy water.

The thickness of each layer provides a clue as to the soil type. For example, the thicker the sand layer, the sandier your soil is. Ideally, you'll want the sand, organic matter, and clay layers to be nearly equal, indicating a loamy soil.

Compost heats up as the organic material biodegrades. This heat kills pathogens and speeds decomposition of the raw materials. While you can throw items into the compost all year, air temperatures must be above 50° F for any real activity to occur. The internal heat within your compost should reach 140° to 150° F. Monitor the temperature in the pile with a large thermometer, which is available at garden centers.

To accelerate the composting process, keep your pile moist, but not wet—a handful should feel like a squeezed-out sponge. Turn your compost with a shovel when it reaches 140° F. Turning encourages the breakdown of organic matter. Speed up the composting process by adding fresh topsoil rich in microorganisms and earthworms or fresh manure. A mix of 50 to 60 percent—by volume and weight—"brown" ingredients (straw, dry leaves) and 50 to 60 percent "green" ingredients (kitchen waste, grass

START WITH THE SOIL
continued

DIGGING CORRECTLY

Breaking new ground is always difficult because of the dense texture of unimproved soil and the presence of rocks, weeds, and tree roots. To reduce the strain on your lower back, take time to dig properly.

First, wear the proper clothes. A pair of heavy boots helps you cut into the soil more efficiently, reducing fatigue. While digging, keep a straight back and good posture. Don't stoop or let your shoulders slump. Also, keep your knees bent at all times. This distributes weight to your legs.

Work when the soil is reasonably moist, but not wet, to minimize the effort of cutting into the earth and the weight of the soil. Scoop only small amounts of soil at a time. Don't load your spade as full as possible each time. Grip the spade far down the handle (close to the blade) to give yourself better control.

clippings) fosters a faster-acting composting process.

How much compost should you apply to the garden? To ensure a level of 5 percent organic matter in your soil, incorporate into the soil about 200 pounds of compost per 50 square feet of garden space each year. Till it into the soil about 1 foot deep.

MANURE: Manure from cows, horses, chickens, sheep, and other plant-eating animals is a great source of nutrients, especially nitrogen, for your plants. Composted or rotted manure is the best because fresh manure can be "hot," meaning it contains such a rich supply of nitrogen that it can overdose your plants and injure or kill them. The injury is called "burning" the plant. If you use fresh manure that has not been composted and you are applying it just before spring planting, try to till it into the soil as early as possible before actually planting the crop.

You can apply fresh manure to the top of the soil in the winter because it will break down before you are ready to till and plant in spring.

Manure is often available free from farms. However, because it hasn't been aged, most manure that comes straight from the farm is more likely to harbor weed seeds than the commercially bagged manure available at most garden centers.

OTHER ORGANIC MATTER: Leaves and grass clippings, old hay and straw, rotted sawdust, and other forms of decaying plant material can be used for organic matter. You may also be able to get waste material, such as peanut or cottonseed hulls, in your area.

COVER CROPS: Even when your garden is lying idle for the winter, you can improve its quality by planting a cover crop. Cover crops not only add nutrients and organic matter to soil, they also help reduce erosion while your vegetable garden is lying idle.

Cover cropping typically is done by planting nutrient-rich plants, such as ryegrass, clover, and vetch, in your garden area during the fall or winter. Most of these crops grow throughout the winter. Many of them are legumes, which fix nitrogen from the air and can add it to the soil as they grow.

Till cover crops into the soil in spring at least three weeks before you plan on planting the garden. This allows the plants to decompose in the soil. Some crops are left until they die, then tilled into the soil. Or you can till them into the soil while they are still lush and green to provide a "green manure" for your garden.

Check with your local extension agent to learn which is the best cover crop for your region and the best way to grow it. In most cases, you reap the benefits by simply broadcasting the seed over areas that have quit producing for the season.

Buckwheat is a warm-weather cover crop. Its roots stretch deep into the soil and improve its texture while the lush foliage chokes out weeds.

Grow annual rye as a winter cover crop. The roots add organic matter to the soil as they decay. You can use the leaves for mulch.

USING FERTILIZERS

Plants need certain nutrients to grow and thrive. They absorb most of these nutrients from the soil through their roots, but sometimes they also take up nutrients through leaves and stems.

The three primary nutrients plants require are nitrogen, phosphorus, and potassium.

NITROGEN: Known as the growth nutrient, plants use nitrogen to develop stocky stems and lush leaves. It keeps plants green and flourishing. A nitrogen-deficient plant has pale, greenish-yellow leaves, and its growth is stunted. Older leaves—the lowest ones on a plant—are the first to show deficiency symptoms. Leafy vegetables, such as cabbage and spinach, are what are known as heavy feeders. They use nitrogen in large amounts. Tomatoes, peppers, and other plants that produce flowers and fruit can get too much nitrogen. When this happens, they grow into huge plants with few flowers and fruit.

PHOSPHORUS: Phosphorus provides energy for plants and promotes root development, growth, and fruiting. A phosphorus-deficient plant is slow growing, stunted, and its leaves may appear dark green, dark blue or reddish.

POTASSIUM: Plants require potassium for vigor and strength. It encourages early root development and increases resistance in the

When side-dressing plants with fertilizer, sprinkle it atop the soil's surface. Then gently mix in the fertilizer without disturbing shallow roots.

plants to certain diseases. It also helps plants tolerate stress from heat and drought. Plants that are deficient in potassium are spindly and poorly developed. They tend to fall over, or lodge easily, and are susceptible to leaf and stem diseases. Severe potassium deficiencies result in leaves curling and browning around the edges starting at the tips, beginning with the leaves lowest on the plant stem and moving up the plant.

MICRONUTRIENTS: These are nutrients, such as sulfur and iron, that plants need in tiny amounts. Generally, micronutrient deficiencies are not common because organic matter and most soils and fertilizers contain sufficient amounts.

UNDERSTANDING pH

An important component of soil fertility is pH, which refers to the acidity or alkalinity of a soil. A neutral pH is 7. Below 7, soil is acidic; above 7, it is alkaline.

Most vegetables grow best with a pH of 6 to 7. In that range, the greatest number of nutrients is available to plants in the highest amounts. However, many plants are adaptable. Asparagus and onions can stand a pH up to 8, while potatoes and radishes tolerate one as low as 4.5.

A pH imbalance can cause crops to take up excess micronutrients, such as magnesium and zinc, or too little of the macronutrients nitrogen, phosphorus, and potassium. Crops then produce poorly and may die. Imbalances also promote some plant diseases. For example, clubroot of cabbage is worse in acid soil than in alkaline soil.

To determine pH, test the soil. The results will tell you how much lime or sulfur to apply. Lime reduces acidity while sulfur increases it; that is, lime raises pH and sulfur lowers it. As a result, plants end up with the proper nutrition.

SYMPTOMS OF NUTRITIONAL DEFICIENCY

When diagnosing a deficiency, keep these points in mind:
■ Not all plants exhibit the same typical symptoms.
■ Not all typical symptoms are due to a deficiency. They may also be caused by diseases, insects, and environmental stresses.
■ If you see symptoms, damage has already occurred.

TYPICAL SYMPTOMS:
■ NITROGEN: Plants grow slowly. Lower leaves are pale green or yellow, later dropping off the plant.
■ PHOSPHORUS: Leaves become unusually dark green. Lower leaves later turn reddish purple.
■ POTASSIUM: The edges of lower leaves turn yellow, then dry up. Sometimes small yellow spots appear on leaf blades.
■ IRON: Upper leaves develop yellowing leaves with veins remaining green. Iron deficiency is common where soil pH is higher than 8 because of the calcium in alkaline soil. It binds with the iron, keeping it in a form that plants can't take up.
■ SULFUR: Leaves over the entire plant turn yellow. They sometimes also take on a beige cast.

USING FERTILIZERS
continued

After planting, water transplants with a dilute solution of liquid fertilizer. Not only does this provide transplanted seedlings with water and nutrients, it helps seedlings off to a fast start because the nutrients in soluble fertilizers are immediately available.

TYPES OF FERTILIZERS

In some areas of the country, such as in the north-central United States, the soil naturally contains enough nutrients to grow a healthy crop. However, this is not the case in most regions. Most likely, you'll need to fertilize.

Fertilizers come in many forms—synthetic and organic, fast-release and slow-release, granular and liquid. They also contain nutrients in a variety of ratios, which are indicated by the three hyphenated numbers on the label (see page 21).

SYNTHETICS: Synthetic fertilizers are manufactured nutrients. These include inexpensive granules that release nutrients as soon as they dissolve and more expensive slow-release formulations that gradually release nutrients throughout the growing season. These materials also come in liquid and water-soluble formulations, which are popular among container gardeners.

While fast-release synthetic fertilizers, such as ammonium nitrate, quickly supply nutrients to plants, they have drawbacks. They tend to be more potent than organic fertilizers and can burn roots and leaves, especially if not watered in. They are highly soluble and may leach into groundwater. If used improperly—applying them in heavy amounts or not watering them in—they may inhibit the activity of soil microbes, decreasing their populations and interfering with the breakdown of organic matter, which, over time, affects soil quality.

ORGANIC FERTILIZERS: Commercial organic or natural fertilizers are made from pelletized fish meal, composted manure, or mixtures of pulverized alfalfa, cottonseed, or other seed meals. You will also find liquid organic formulations, such as fish emulsion, which can be mixed with water and poured over the roots of your crop.

Each type of organic fertilizer has its advantages and disadvantages; some are more appropriate for certain situations than others. Blood meal, for example, is an excellent source of nitrogen, but it doesn't supply phosphorus or potassium. Dried cow manure provides nitrogen and improves soil structure, but if it's not composted, it can burn plants.

Composted organic fertilizers don't have specific application rates. That's not a problem. Because their nutrients are less concentrated, you can apply excessive, unmeasured amounts without harming plants. In addition, organic fertilizers help build soil.

Organic and slow-release synthetic fertilizers rely on microorganisms in the soil

KEY TO FERTILIZER INGREDIENTS

SYNTHETIC-INORGANIC MATERIALS:
- Water soluble
- Rapid plant response
- Effects last 2 to 6 weeks
- Can leach through soil
- Can burn plants

Examples include ammonium nitrate, ammonium sulfate, calcium nitrate, and sodium nitrate.

NATURAL-ORGANIC MATERIALS:
- Not water soluble
- Slow plant response
- Effects last 4 to 8 weeks
- Nitrogen release is by microbial activity and so soil temperatures must be 55° F or above.
- Does not leach through soil or burn plants.

Examples include activated sewage sludge, composted manures, bone meal, cottonseed meal, fish emulsion.

SYNTHETIC ORGANICS:
- Not water soluble
- Effects last 8 weeks or more
- May or may not burn plants
- Nitrogen release is by microbial activity
- Unlikely to leach through soil.

Examples include urea (burns plants), ureaformaldehyde, IBDU, sulfur- and plastic-coated urea, and methylene urea.

to break down and release nutrients. For that reason, their nutrients are available to plants gradually rather than all at once—a benefit. However, plants are at the mercy of whatever affects the microbes. For example, fungi and bacteria are not active in cold weather or dry soil, which means plants will go without nutrients under these conditions.

Over the long term, organic fertilizers are a splendid source of nutrients for vegetables. But if a crop is showing signs of nutrient deficiency, an organic fertilizer would not be the choice for a quick fix.

NUTRIENT RATIOS: The three hyphenated numbers you see on fertilizer bags indicate the ratio of the nitrogen-, phosphorus-, and potassium-supplying materials inside. A balanced fertilizer, such as 10-10-10, contains equal amounts of each of these nutrients (a ratio of 1:1:1). Choose the fertilizer with the ratio indicated by soil test results.

APPLYING FERTILIZER

When fertilizing vegetables, start with an initial dose based on soil test results, mixing it into the soil before planting the garden. This initial application corrects any soil deficiencies.

Never exceed recommended rates on the fertilizer package. Overapplying fertilizer is a waste of time and money and may harm both your crops—by burning leaves and roots—and the environment—by polluting the water supply. It also causes plants such as tomatoes to grow abundant foliage, but no fruit.

Spread dry fertilizers over the garden. Then, incorporate them into the top 6 to 10 inches of soil by scratching them in or by irrigating to dissolve the fertilizer. You can also "feed" as you plant by mixing a slow-release fertilizer with the backfill.

Depending on the kind of fertilizer you use, the type of soil in the garden, and the crops you grow, you may need to fertilize several times a season. For example, most fast-release fertilizers are available to plants for only two to four weeks. Any nutrients the plants miss washes beyond plant-root reach. Sandy soil is infertile and requires frequent fertilizing. And some crops are heavy feeders, while others often need a boost during certain stages of growth, such as when sweet corn forms ears.

Using a slow-release synthetic fertilizer, which can provide nutrients for eight weeks to nine months depending on type, eliminates the need to fertilize more than once.

To make midseason applications of quick-release materials, sidedress the plants. Scratch the fertilizer into the soil around their base or along the row, then water them in to prevent burning. You can also spray plants with liquid and water-soluble fertilizers. Apply them directly to the crop or pour them over plant roots. Time the applications for early morning, early evening, or a cloudy day. Water evaporates more slowly at these times, and so the crop absorbs more nutrients.

Another quick boost for plants is to make a nutrient "tea." Combine one part manure or compost with three parts water. Place the manure in a cloth bag in the bottom of a 30-gallon garbage can. Add the water, let steep for 24 hours, then pour the tea around the base of plants.

Pay attention to plants' nutritional needs. Start by preparing soil well, mixing in plenty of organic matter. Fertilize plants as needed to take care of any temporary deficiencies. Then your garden will be as healthy, productive, and pest free as this one.

LENGTH OF DAYS

The farther away from the equator, the longer the summer day. For plants, this can have a big effect on productivity. Take spinach as an example. It's a long-day plant and when days last 13 hours, they flower, set seed, and stop leaf production. Short of completely blocking their light, there's no way to keep spinach from doing this when days are long.

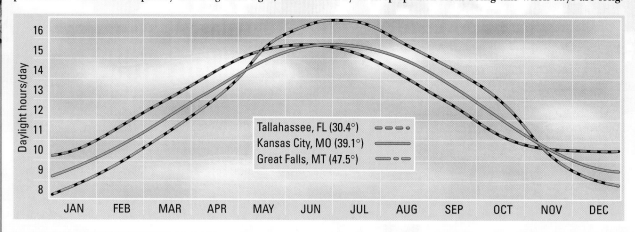

Daylight hours/day

Tallahassee, FL (30.4°)
Kansas City, MO (39.1°)
Great Falls, MT (47.5°)

JAN FEB MAR APR MAY JUN JUL AUG SEP OCT NOV DEC

GARDENING WITH THE SEASONS

Vegetable gardens change with the seasons, so planting is a continual process. Cool-season crops like cabbage and lettuce take center stage in spring, followed by warm-season squash and tomatoes in summer. Fall brings a second chance for vegetables that like cool weather, including kale, spinach, and other plants that can survive winter's chill.

Garden planning, cultivating, planting, and harvesting can keep you busy all year. Making efficient use of each season will help you improve the quality of your vegetables, extend your gardening season to its limits, and sustain your gardening passion.

Matching crops to the appropriate season or using season-stretching techniques can keep you in produce for many months. Even in winter, you can be productive by starting transplants and ordering seeds. This chapter will jump-start the learning process to help you make the most of the entire gardening year.

MATCHING CROPS TO SEASONS

Vegetables usually are divided into two categories—cool- and warm-season crops. Whether you live in a cool or warm region, you should be able to grow both kinds. The trick is timely planting and successive gardening, which allow you to plant cool-season crops early in the year, follow them with warm-season crops for in the summer garden, and then replant cool-season crops for fall and winter.

COOL-SEASON VEGETABLES: Many plants of European origin, such as lettuce and cabbage, thrive in cool weather. Cool-season vegetables grow best when temperatures range between 40° and 75° F. In most areas, cool-season crops can be planted two to four weeks before the last spring frost. They will stop producing in early summer when daytime temperatures reach 80° F and higher. In regions where nights remain cool, you can make small, successive sowings throughout summer.

In hotter regions, plant cool-season vegetables as early as possible in spring and replant them for fall. There also are cold-hardy vegetables that can survive throughout winter in most regions. These include carrots, root crops, onions, and artichokes.

WARM-SEASON VEGETABLES: Warm-season vegetables, such as tomatoes, peppers, corn, and okra, originated in tropical climates. They are killed by a frost, and they won't germinate or perform well if temperatures fall below 50° F.

You can sustain many warm-season crops into fall if you protect them from frosts and freezes with cold frames, row covers, or other season-extending devices. But they perform best during the height of summer.

PREPARING FOR SPRING

For many gardeners, winter may be excruciating, especially if warm snaps tempt you into believing that spring has sprung. But it's unwise to plant many crops until the ground is warm and dry and the probability of a late freeze is past. Yet, there are ways to "garden" in the winter. Peruse seed catalogs and make plans. If ordering seeds, do so in January or February. Many spring crops can be seeded inside starting in mid-February.

SOWING SEED INDOORS

Sowing seeds indoors in late winter offers several advantages. It allows you to spring into the gardening season early by growing your own transplants. Often homegrown seedlings are healthier and more robust because you have control over their growing conditions.

CONTAINERS: You can use a variety of containers for sowing seed. Peat pots, compressed peat pellets, plastic pots, and fiber blocks are available at garden centers. Salad-bar packages, egg cartons, and other recyclables work just as well. No matter what you use, the container must have good drainage.

SOIL: The growing medium—potting soil—in which the seeds are planted should drain well, have adequate water-holding capacity, and be free of contaminants. You can make your own by mixing sand and organic matter with sterilized topsoil and nutrients. However, for most gardeners, it's easier to buy soil that's commercially made. One cubic foot of potting soil should fill about 275 2¼-inch-square pots.

SOWING: Before planting the seedlings, fill the container with growing medium, and water it well. Allow it to drain overnight. Plant seeds about 1 inch apart in the trays. If you are using a large, undivided seedling flat, an easy way to make "rows" is to take a narrow board and press it into the medium forming a trench about 1 inch deep. Drop the seeds into the trench and cover with medium.

WATERING: Place a watertight tray or pan beneath your container and water plants from the bottom, keeping about ¼ to ½ inch of water in the tray at all times.

VEGETABLES FOR SPRING GARDENS

SOW AND GROW IN COOL SPRING SOIL:

Arugula	Mustard
Beets	Parsley
Carrots	Parsnip
Chard	Peas
Kohlrabi	Potato
Lettuce	Radish
Mesclun	Spinach

START INDOORS AND TRANSPLANT IN MID TO LATE SPRING:

Artichokes	Eggplant
Broccoli	Onions
Cabbage	Peppers
Celery	Tomatoes
Chinese cabbage	

PERENNIALS TO HARVEST IN SPRING:

Asparagus	Rhubarb

NO-CHILL SEEDLINGS

Some cool-season vegetables require protection from exposure to chilly temperatures below 40° F. If chilled for more than a week, celery, Chinese cabbage, and other cool-season vegetables such as spinach respond by producing flowers and seeds. This process, called bolting, also is encouraged by rapidly lengthening days. Bolting is never a problem when these sensitive vegetables are grown in the fall, when days are shorter.

SEED STARTING

Start seeds in clean containers filled with a sterile soilless mix, available in bags at garden centers. Fill containers to the top and dampen them well before you plant the seeds.

Cover the seeded containers with plastic to keep the surface constantly moist. Keep them in a warm place and provide strong light as soon as sprouts appear.

LIGHT: Place seedlings near a window that faces south or southwest in a room that has a nighttime temperature of no more than 60° F. Cool nights tend to make seedlings stockier and more robust. Most vegetable seeds will sprout at room temperature (about 70° F), but some plants, such as peppers, cabbages, and tomatoes, will germinate much faster if given slightly warmer temperatures. To increase warmth, place seedling containers on a heating pad that has been set on its lowest temperature. Shut off the pad at night.

Typically, there isn't enough natural late-winter light to grow seedlings on a windowsill. If you're growing seedlings where light is limited, use cool-white fluorescent grow lights. Place the lights about 2 inches above plants, raising them as plants grow. Plants that have to stretch toward light tend to have long, flimsy stems, which are easily damaged and may be too weak to support foliage and fruit. Provide 12 to 14 hours of light per day.

In warmer regions, you can grow seedlings outside in protected areas or in cold frames.

THINNING: When plants are about 1 inch tall and before the first true leaves develop, thin them to no more than three strong seedlings per 2-inch pot. When seedlings first emerge, they typically have two small, delicate leaves. A third leaf, their first "true" leaf, emerges as they mature. This leaf is usually larger, has a different shape, and is more vigorous than the seedling leaves.

FERTILIZING: Most planting media does not contain enough nutrients to support plants through the seedling stage, so use a water-soluble fertilizer that has been diluted with twice the amount of water shown on the label. Use this solution in place of plain water after plants have formed their first true leaf and continue watering with it every 7 to 10 days. If fertilizer sticks to the leaves, rinse the seedlings with plain water.

DAMPING OFF: Some seedlings may develop problems as they mature. Soil-borne fungi can cause a root disease known as "damping off," which causes seedlings to fall over and die. Prevent this by using a sterile medium. Also, allow the soil surface to dry before watering.

INSECTS: You may also have problems with insects. Often, pests come from nearby plants, so try to be sure the growing area is pest free. Pesticides or insecticidal soaps can be used. Be sure to follow label directions for spraying seedlings.

HARDENING OFF: Before transplanting seedlings into the garden, prepare them for the outdoors by "hardening off." To do this, reduce the growing temperature, withhold water, and increase the light intensity.

An easy way to harden off seedlings is to set them outside in mild weather during the last two to three weeks before planting in the garden. Bring plants back indoors if frost is expected. Water them when the surface of the medium dries out.

HANDLING PURCHASED PLANTS

When buying vegetables as bedding plants, look for small young seedlings. Pick up the flat or pot to see if roots are wandering out through the drainage holes. Excessive root growth is a good indicator of advanced age.

As soon as you buy them, either set out plants in the garden or move them to larger containers. Squeeze seedlings from containers rather than pulling on them. Spread the lowest roots slightly to help them break out of the circular pattern that often develops in containers. A cloche (see page 26) will help ease the transition of greenhouse-grown seedlings to the garden.

Thin seedlings so they are at least 2 inches apart. Pull out tiny seedlings with tweezers or use small sharp scissors to clip them off at the soil line. Keep the soil evenly moist.

Move seedlings outdoors gradually, taking care to protect them from strong winds. Or, harden off seedlings by moving them to a well-ventilated cold frame for one to two weeks.

SEASON-STRETCHING DEVICES

Peppers benefit from the warmth and wind protection provided by milk-carton cloches. Cloches also prevent damage from heavy rain or hail.

You can harden off seedlings in a cold frame. On sunny days, open the cover to prevent overheating the plants.

In addition to starting seeds indoors, many gardeners use special devices to grow plants outside before the weather warms up. These devices include cloches, cold frames, and plastic tunnels.

The sooner you get plants into the garden the better they will grow and the sooner they will produce fruit. All of these devices help protect crops from cold weather and cold soils early in the season.

CLOCHES: Cloches fit over the top of plants to form mini-greenhouses. Gallon-size plastic milk jugs work as well as commercial glass or plastic cloches.

To make a milk-carton cloche, remove the jug's bottom and cut a V-shaped slit in the top of the handle. Place a jug over each plant and push a straight stick through the handle and into the ground deeply enough to firmly anchor the jug in the soil. Leave caps off the jugs unless freezing weather is expected, and remove the jugs on warm days (50° to 60° F) to prevent excessive heat buildup. Otherwise the plants could "cook" in the cloche. Replace the jugs if a cold snap is forecast.

COLD FRAMES: Cold frames are boxes with translucent tops that you place over a garden area. They can be permanent or moveable. They allow the sun in and keep cold winds out. Cold frames are available commercially, or you can build one using lumber for the sides and corrugated fiberglass for the top. Recycled building materials, such as cement blocks and old windows, also make fine, low-cost cold frames. Simply set windows on blocks placed around your crop. Or use straw bales for the walls.

The translucent top of a cold frame creates a greenhouse effect. Heat will build up inside the frame on sunny days, so be sure your cold frame is easy to ventilate. On warm days, remove or lift the lid to let air in, then close it again at night or if a freeze is expected.

TUNNELS: Plastic tunnels work much like cold frames. To set them up, cut support hoops of 10-gauge wire or ½-inch bendable pipe into

Floating row covers, plastic tunnels, and wire cylinders wrapped in plastic provide extra warmth in the spring garden.

pieces long enough to arch 14 to 18 inches over your beds or rows. Six-foot-long supports fit perfectly over 3-foot-wide beds. Push the hoops at least 2 inches into the ground on each side of the row. Space them 2 feet apart.

Cover supports with clear plastic sheeting (2 mils thick) and secure the edges to the ground with bricks, cement blocks, or landscape timbers. Cut vents in the plastic to allow heat to escape and reinforce the vents with duct tape to prevent them from tearing. Remove the tunnels when spring temperatures consistently reach 60° to 70° F. Make sure that you regularly water plants growing under cold frames and tunnels so that they don't dry out.

ROW COVERS: Although they lack the greenhouse properties of the other season extenders, row covers also protect vegetables in cool weather. They warm the row 2 to 3° F compared to surrounding air, which often is enough to save crops from a late frost.

SPRING PLANTING

You can plant seeds and transplants directly into the ground when soil reaches about 60° F and is fairly dry. It is dry enough to plant if you can press a handful of it in your fist and then readily crumble it into smaller bits.

Before planting, loosen the soil by tilling or turning it with a long-handled garden fork. Topsoil should be finely textured and free of large clods. This allows sprouts to push through the soil surface, and water and fertilizer to seep into the root zone. After tilling shape soil into rows or beds.

SOWING SEEDS DIRECTLY

When planting seeds directly into soil, dig a furrow in the middle of the row with a hoe or trowel. For straight rows, run a plumb line from two stakes located at the end of each row as a guide. Cover small seeds, such as lettuce and carrots, with a scant ¼ inch of soil; larger seeds, such as corn and beans, with an inch or more of soil.

Water your garden gently as soon as the seeds are planted. This is one situation when short, shallow watering is good for your crop. Soil should be moist but not wet. Use a fine mist so that you don't wash away or compact

You'll get a better stand of seedlings if you cover seeds with screened compost or other loose, organic material. The compost won't form a crust over seeds, as soil might, and it holds moisture well.

the soil. Watch the garden daily to make sure soil stays moist around the seeds until they have emerged and look vigorous. Apply a thin layer of light mulch, such as straw, over seeded beds to retain moisture. Remove it gently as soon as seedlings begin to emerge so that they can get full sun.

Some seeds simply will not germinate, which is why you should initially plant them close together. Thin them to their proper spacing when they are 1 to 2 inches tall. Grab seedlings by the stem and close to the soil surface so you remove them by their roots. If you're dealing with many tiny seedlings, such as lettuce, use a table fork to lift them.

If nothing emerges from a planting, you may have planted seeds too deeply or a crust may have formed over a slow-to-germinate vegetable. It is also possible you have a batch of old, nonviable seed. The seeds from some vegetables, such as okra and beans, remain viable for years if stored correctly, but other crop seeds, such as onion and lettuce, have a shelf life of three years or less. Make sure you purchase seed from a reliable dealer and store them according to package directions.

Before direct-sowing large dry seeds, such as sweet corn, beans, peas, or okra, soak them in water for a few hours or overnight.

TRANSPLANTING

Prepare the soil for transplants by tilling and cultivating so that the top 4 inches or more is finely textured and free of clods. Spread fertilizer over the soil or mix it directly into furrows or planting holes. Water well after transplanting to keep the fertilizer from burning tender roots.

If using purchased transplants, buy young seedlings. Pick up the flat and examine the base for roots growing out the drainage holes. Excessive root growth indicates older plants. Set transplants in the garden as soon as you buy them, or move them to larger containers if you can't plant within a few days after buying.

Plant most seedlings at the same depth as they grew in the pot. Some vegetables, such as tomatoes, do better planted deeper. They grow roots on the buried stem, which helps stabilize them. Gently loosen pot-bound roots so they don't continue growing in a circle.

SUMMERTIME

Life becomes hectic in the garden during the summer as crops mature, weeds take off, and insects become more prevalent. This is also when spring crops begin to wane and summer crops take their place. If growing summer crops from seed, sow them directly into the garden. Remember, they will germinate and grow more rapidly than their spring cousins, so keep a close eye on them for thinning, spacing, and watering.

Summer transplants may need help adjusting to the heat. If temperatures are extremely hot (more than 80° F), shade plants with a pot, cardboard box, or row cover the first few days after transplanting. This allows seedlings to concentrate on growing roots rather than coping with heat and bright sunshine.

Summer crops generally grow much larger than spring crops, so make sure you leave enough room for them to grow. When irrigating in summer, be sure to give the soil a deep soaking. Summer is a good time to switch to drip irrigation because you'll lose less water to evaporation.

After planting, apply additional mulch to keep soil cool and help it retain water, as well as to control weeds. Spread it about 2 inches deep around the plants.

MANAGING PESTS

Insects can be a problem at any time, but in summer they are particularly troublesome. Early intervention and constant vigilance is the key to controlling pests. Examine plants for signs of damage. Vary the times when you look for pests, because different insects are active at different times of day. Slugs, beetles, and caterpillars feed at night, and flying insects are more active during the day.

A few holes in your leaves are rarely a problem. But significant damage, or a large population of insects, needs immediate action. The most notorious garden insect pests are described in Chapter 4, paired with the plants they are most likely to attack. You can collect samples of insects and their damage for your local extension agent or garden center staff to identify. Control measures include covering plants with row covers, hand-picking pests, encouraging beneficial insects, and spraying insecticides.

VEGETABLES FOR SUMMER GARDENS

SOW AND GROW IN WARM SUMMER SOIL:

Basil	Okra
Beans	Peanuts
Cantaloupe	Pumpkins
Corn	Squash
Cucumbers	Watermelons

TRANSPLANT TO GARDEN IN SUMMER:

Eggplant	Peppers
Jerusalem artichokes	Tomatoes

Edible signet marigolds (Tagetes tenuifolia) enrich gardens with color, and their fragrant foliage provides habitat for beneficial insects. Onions and herbs also deter garden pests, which are always most active during the long, warm days of summer.

Lightweight row covers form a barrier that pests cannot penetrate, yet water and sunlight pass right through them. Secure the edges to keep insects from sneaking inside. Keep the covers loose so that vegetables underneath have room to grow.

Filtered shade safeguards the flavor and quality of lettuce and other cool-season crops after the weather turns hot. In summer, you can also use a wood lath like this one to shade newly planted beds.

PROTECTING GOOD BUGS

Some insects encountered in the garden are beneficial. Ladybugs, spiders, lacewings, and some wasps control a wide variety of destructive insects. Luring them into your garden is easy and wise. Flowers with tiny blossoms, such as yarrow and Queen Anne's lace, provide habitat. Clovers and such herbs as basil, rosemary, and tansy also encourage their presence. Other flowers and herbs actually repel insect pests. For example, onions and garlic interspersed in the garden help control aphids, and marigolds planted in large numbers can repel a variety of insect pests.

POLLINATION

Most vegetables, except leafy greens and root crops, form fruit from flowers, which means they must be pollinated to produce a crop. Often nature takes care of everything. Some crops are self-fertile (neighboring plants share pollen) and some are self-sterile (they must be pollinated by another variety). In addition, some plants can pollinate themselves. But other vegetables need an outside agent, such as wind or insects, to transfer pollen.

Don't spray insecticides when crops are flowering, because they also kill pollinating insects. If using a row cover, lift it occasionally to give pollinating insects access to your crop. Tomatoes, beans, and corn often benefit from a little human intervention for pollination. Gently shake their stems occasionally to spread the pollen. Also, planting corn in blocks, instead of in single rows, enhances pollination.

Crops may drop their flowers before pollination occurs during hot weather. For example, tomatoes don't set fruit when temperatures rise above 90° F. You can shade plants with sheets or light-filtering fabric. Lay the covers across the crops or stake them above plants during the hottest hours. But also be patient. When mild weather returns, most crops will start producing again.

MAINTENANCE CHECKLIST

- Harvest ripe vegetables.
- Weed and thin plants as needed.
- Patrol for pests.
- Mulch exposed ground.
- Stake tall vegetables; trellis vines.
- Fertilize as needed.
- Provide water before the soil dries out.
- Pull up spent crops promptly.

Tomatoes, peppers, and beans may fail to set fruit in hot weather despite having flowers. Heat kills the pollen. Pollination problems should end when cool weather returns.

FALL GARDENS

Cool-season vegetables, such as leaf lettuce, round out the growing year. Plant them in late summer to harvest until frost.

For most areas of the country, fall is yet another growing season. Many cool-season crops thrive in the cooler autumn temperatures, and some crops even taste better in fall than in spring.

The biggest challenge for a fall garden is getting crops into the ground early enough to produce before a freeze, but not so early that summer heat reduces their output. Fall crops often take longer to reach maturity (as much as three weeks longer) than those planted in spring, which makes timing planting somewhat more challenging.

Some cool-season crops, such as brussels sprouts, spinach, and mesclun can take a bit of frost. Others, such as leeks, carrots, and parsnips, can be harvested well into November and December. For most crops, though, you want them to bear fruit before that first frost.

Use the date of your area's first predicted frost to estimate planting schedules. Add 21 days to the estimated days to maturity on your seed package, then count back from the frost date to establish a planting date. Add an additional two weeks to this figure for fall plantings of warm-

season vegetables, such as bush beans, cucumbers, and squash.

Some cool-season vegetable seeds will not sprout in the heat of summer, so consider sowing these seeds indoors and transplanting them to the garden when they are about one month old.

GARDENING WITH FROST

Many warm-season crops will be damaged by light frost, but you can protect these crops by covering them with blankets during early, mild frosts. Remove the blankets the next morning or when warmer weather returns. And don't expect too much of warm-season crops as fall progresses. They hardly grow once night temperatures reach 55° F or less.

Cool-season crops often taste better after a light frost, and exposing them to early frosts will help prepare them for the harder freezes to come in fall and winter. However, if frigid temperatures should arrive suddenly, cover crops with light blankets or cardboard boxes to protect them from extreme changes. Also, water crops thoroughly on the eve of a hard freeze because saturated soil freezes more slowly than dry soil.

Don't assume that cold-hardy vegetables are dead just because they've been frozen. All of the cold-hardy plants listed in the box on page 31 can recover from a hard freeze. However, they all will also look and taste better and be less susceptible to cold-season problems, such as downy mildew and root rot,

VEGETABLES FOR FALL GARDENS

SOW IN LATE SUMMER:

Arugula	Lettuce
Carrots	Mesclun
Chard	Mustard
Fennel	Radishes
Kale	Spinach
Kohlrabi	Turnips

TRANSPLANT IN LATE SUMMER:

Broccoli	Chinese cabbage
Brussels sprouts	Parsley
Cabbage	Scallions
Cauliflower	

if you grow them in cold frames or under tunnels during winter.

MOVING ON AND CLEANING UP

As crop production wanes, it's tempting to leave plants in the garden just so you can harvest one last tomato or pepper from the plant. You would be better served if you remove waning crops and replace them with new cool-season ones. This will help you extend the current growing season and provide fresh options for the coming spring.

When crops wither and die, remove them from the garden. Dead crop residue provides a home where pests and diseases overwinter. Pull plants up by the roots and chop them if you're throwing them into the compost heap. If plants were diseased or insect infested, throw them into the trash rather than on the compost pile so that you don't harbor problems. You can also rototill spent plants into the garden, but don't do so unless you're positive the plants were healthy.

In late fall, prepare the garden by turning under any old mulch and digging out persistent weeds. Spread a fresh supply of mulch—fallen leaves, for example—over the clean garden, or plant winter cover crops. Fall is a great time to improve your soil by

incorporating organic matter because the soil usually contains just the right amount of moisture for tilling and it's still warm enough to be outside.

In cold climates, mulch around cold-hardy vegetables, such as carrots, Jerusalem artichokes, and root crops to give them added winter protection.

Clean, sharpen, and protect garden equipment before putting it away for winter. Spray metal parts with a metal protector or coat them with oil, treating wooden handles, too. Before storing cold frames, wire cages, and other structures, wash them thoroughly to remove disease organisms or chemical residues.

Light frost improves the flavor of many cool-season crops such as this 'Super Dome' broccoli. In late summer, plant leafy greens, cabbage-family crops, and root vegetables such as parsnips, carrots, and rutabagas so that they mature around the time of the first frost.

LOOKING AHEAD

As you clean up, begin thinking ahead to the coming season. Plan crop rotations, outline strategies for improving soil, and study your diary to decide what changes you'll make next season. Your diary should be your memory. Jot notes as you grow; you'll be glad you did.

You can dig carrots and parsnips out of the garden all winter if you mulch them well to keep the soil around them from freezing. Mark the location of these buried treasures before they are covered with snow.

COLD-HARDY VEGETABLES

Brussels sprouts	Mâche
Cabbage	Parsley
Garlic	Spinach
Kale	
Lettuce (some varieties)	

GROWING GREAT VEGETABLES

As you read these pages, you'll find it helpful to keep the following points in mind. Unless specifically spelled out for a crop, these guidelines apply to all vegetables.

■ Assume a soil pH of 6.2 to 6.8 unless otherwise indicated.

■ See individual entries for a vegetable's ideal site considerations. However, many crops tolerate a range of conditions. The important point to remember is that all vegetables do better if the soil is well-prepared, fertile, and well-drained.

■ If a spacing range is provided (for example, space cabbage transplants 18 to 24 inches apart), plant smaller varieties at the closer spacing (18 to 21 inches), larger cultivars at the wider spacing (21 to 24 inches).

■ Keep in mind that you don't have to plant in rows, even though row spacings are given for each crop. Seeds such as spinach or lettuce can be broadcast in patches; you can plant many others in blocks, squares, double rows, etc.

■ Use floating row covers—the lightest weight available—at planting

From start to finish, the life of a vegetable is a continuous rush to reproduce. First the seed swells and the first curls of root and leaf emerge. The sprout orients itself to sun and earth, and develops its first green leaves. Growing larger each day, plants prepare themselves to flower. Pollen carried on the wind travels to waiting silks below. After a few short weeks, succulent sweet corn is ready for harvest.

to exclude insects pests, such as flea beetles, leafminers, Colorado potato beetles, cabbageworms and loopers, carrot rust flies and maggots, and cucumber beetles. Loosely lay the cover over plants; tuck its edges into the soil with a shovel, leaving no openings. Remove the cover when you weed and when insect-pollinated vegetables, such as cucumbers, bloom so that pollinators can get to the flowers.

■ Remove spent plants at the end of the growing season to eliminate the overwintering sites of pests. Throw plants on the compost pile.

■ Always read fungicide and insecticide labels, to be sure a pesticide product is approved for use on the intended crop and that the pesticide will actually control the pest that's causing problems. Be sure to check the rate to use, too.

■ Hose off small populations of soft-bodied insects, such as aphids, with a sharp stream of water. The bacteria Bacillus thuringiensis (Bt) helps control the larvae of pests such as cabbage loopers and corn earworms.

■ Rotate crops to aid disease control.

MATURATION TIMES

Catalogs and seed packets usually list the estimated days from seeding or transplanting until the first fruit is mature and ready to pick. For transplants such as tomatoes and peppers, count from the day you set out the plants. When seeding, count from the day you sow the seeds.

Cool temperatures, persistent cloud cover, or shortening autumn days can slow the maturation of many plants. Warmth, sun, and lengthening spring days usually make vegetables grow faster. Days to harvest also depends on cultivars. A range is shown for many of the vegetables on these pages.

■ The varieties listed for each vegetable in this encyclopedia are dependable and easy to grow. But the world is full of wonderful varieties whose flavors, colors, and tolerance to growing conditions vary radically. Experiment to find the ones right for your taste and garden.

Supermarket shelves offer a small sample of the vast world of vegetables. Growing your own may be the only way to taste unusual varieties, such as this crinkled 'Lacinato' kale. To experience rare taste treats, try unusual varieties of tomatoes and other common vegetables.

ARTICHOKES
Cynara scolymus

ARTICHOKE FACTS

Site: Full sun. Well-drained rich soil. Moist, protected. Small amounts of nitrogen fertilizer mixed into soil before planting.
Planting: Plant root divisions after last frost.
Spacing: 2–3 feet apart in rows 2½–3 feet apart.
Harvest: Late summer. Leave an inch of stem.
Storage: Refrigerate in a plastic bag for up to two weeks. Days to harvest: 90–100 from transplanting.

The grayish foliage of artichokes accents gardens with its unusual texture. The plants are perennial in mild winter climates.

ABOUT ARTICHOKES

Artichokes are thistles without the sting. Both the tender hearts of their large buds and the bases of their thick scales are edible.

Where winters are mild (zone 7) and summers are cool and foggy, artichokes are short-lived perennials. Expect them to bear well for three or four years. In northern areas, where cold winters usually kill plants, grow artichokes as annuals. Plants are most productive in cool, damp summers. Annual artichokes may grow a dozen buds or none at all, depending on the weather. But even when they never set a bud, their spiky, gray-green leaves are a pretty garden sight.

GROWING ARTICHOKES

Six weeks before your last frost, plant three seeds in 4-inch pots filled with sterile potting soil. Keep the containers moist and warm until sprouts appear. Then immediately move the seedlings to strong light. Two weeks after germination, pull out all but the strongest seedling from each pot.

After all danger of frost is passed, transplant the seedlings into a garden site with rich, well-drained soil, spacing them 2 to 3 feet apart. Handle the seedlings gently, without disturbing the roots. Keep the soil constantly moist for the next two weeks or until the plants become established.

Expect fast growth as long as nights remain cool and slower growth in hot summer weather. When nights cool again in late summer, flower buds develop atop stout stems. Cut them when they are at least 3 inches in diameter, taking a 1-inch stub of stem with each bud. You can refrigerate the harvest for up to two weeks.

In zones 7 and 8, artichokes overwinter in the ground if protected. Before the first freeze, cut plants back to about 10 inches and mulch the crowns with a 12-inch-deep mound of clean hay or small leaves. Then cover the mulched crowns with an old blanket or cardboard box.

Remove the winter protection in spring when small tufts of leaves emerge from the old crown. Your plants have survived. Fertilize them with a 1-inch mulch of rotted manure and a light application of a balanced fertilizer.

One-, two-, and three-year-old plants will produce a good crop of buds in early summer. After harvesting, prune plants back by a third to encourage a second "flowering" in fall.

In addition to sowing seeds, you can propagate artichokes vegetatively. Use a sharp knife to cut off the healthiest tufts of leaves that appear around the old crowns in spring, and transplant them immediately.

SELECTIONS

In areas where artichokes grow as perennials, varieties such as purple-tinged 'Violetto' are worth a try in your garden, and 'Green Globe Improved' is productive and good tasting. For growing as an annual, the top choice is 'Imperial Star'.

Artichokes are grown for the tender fleshy hearts found in the base of immature flower buds. Although they are related to thistles, their leaves don't develop prickles.

ARUGULA
Eruca sativa

For the best flavor, pick the young inner leaves from arugula plants. Older leaves often have a sharp, bitter tang.

ABOUT ARUGULA

Arugula is a gourmet green that is often expensive to buy yet incredibly easy to grow.

Also known as roquette or rocket, arugula has a rich, full-bodied addictive flavor. Young, tender leaves are delicious in salads or on sandwiches, or you can lightly braise them with whole garlic cloves and enjoy them as a cooked vegetable. Flowers are edible, too.

For best flavor, grow arugula in cool weather and harvest only the youngest leaves. Heat makes older leaves taste sharply bitter.

GROWING ARUGULA

Because arugula grows fast and the youngest leaves are the best for eating, plant it twice a year, in spring and late summer. Just before your last spring frost, sow seeds 1 inch apart in rows or broadcast them in small patches, barely covering them with soil.

You can also start arugula indoors four weeks before the average date of the last spring frost. Whether growing seedlings indoors or out, water plants regularly to help them grow quickly. In moist soil, seeds germinate in three to six days.

Begin harvesting arugula leaves four to six weeks after sowing seed by pinching off young, 4-inch-long leaves from the centers of the plants. You also can gather arugula by the handful, cutting the leaves 2 inches above the ground with a sharp knife or scissors.

Thoroughly water plants after a heavy cutting, and they will quickly produce a new crop of tender young leaves for you to enjoy.

Tiny flea beetles often feed on arugula in late spring, chewing numerous small holes in the leaves. Floating row covers are the best way to protect plants from their damage.

Pull up spring-sown arugula when the weather turns hot and the leaves become bitter, or let a few plants flower and shed seeds. Volunteer seedlings often appear as autumn brings cool weather.

Arugula planted in late summer holds its flavor much longer than plants grown in spring. Sow fall crop six weeks before the first frost.

As your plants gain size, thin them, harvesting the small inner leaves for salads and larger outer leaves for cooking. Or you can pull up entire plants until the seedlings are spaced about 4 inches apart.

This vegetable easily tolerates light frosts. You can continue to pick leaves through early winter if you cover your fall crop with plastic tunnels, which will protect the plants to at least 20° F. If some plants survive winter, cut them back to within 2 inches of the crown in early spring to force out a final flush of new leaves before the plants flower.

SELECTIONS

Seed companies sell vigorous strains that have been selected from wild plants found in Europe. Mature leaves may be as much as 10 inches long and are dark green with round, lobed edges. 'Sylvetta' has smaller leaves, white veins, and much stronger flavor. It is also more bolt resistant than other varieties.

ARUGULA FACTS

Site: Full sun to part shade. Rich soil. Tolerates dry sites and frost.
Planting: By seed in spring 4–6 weeks before average last frost, or in late summer for fall crop.
Spacing: ¼ inch deep, 2 inches apart, rows 12 inches apart. Thin plants to 8 inches apart when they are 3–4 inches tall.
Care: Benefits from side dressing of compost or well-rotted manure. Water during drought. Remove and discard flower stalks as they appear.
Harvest: Leaves as desired or remove whole plants at ground level with a sharp knife. Eat the thinnings.
Peculiarities: Prone to bolting in heat; avoid by selecting bolt-resistant varieties. No major pests or diseases.

Frequent harvesting keeps arugula plants productive for a long time. You can pick leaves individually, or shear back the plants to promote tender new leaves. If you allow the plants to flower, their lavender blossoms are also edible.

ASPARAGUS
Asparagus officinalis

ABOUT ASPARAGUS

The most enduring vegetable you can grow in your garden, asparagus can furnish tender spears, or stems, for 10, 20, or even 30 years. Dense circular crowns of long, fleshy roots send up more spears than the plant can use, so there is no harm in harvesting them for up to six weeks each spring. From late spring to fall, allow the plants to grow freely; they will die back completely in winter, having stored up plenty of strength for the following year's harvest.

Asparagus grows in zones 4 to 8, but it will not produce well in more temperate zones where the winters are so short and mild that the plants never become completely dormant.

Harvest when spears are 10 inches long or less. Check the asparagus bed daily because the stems toughen and the tips leaf out within a week.

Asparagus spears push through to the surface in early spring. The spears are young leaf stalks that grow from the roots.

GROWING ASPARAGUS

Carefully choose a garden site for asparagus because it will be there a long time. Its site should be well-drained and enriched with plenty of organic matter. Add lime to raise the pH to 6.5 or higher, if necessary.

You can start some asparagus varieties from seed, but you will gain one to two years of harvesting time by starting with dormant roots, which are called crowns.

Buy crowns in late winter or early spring, and plant them 14 inches apart in a well-cultivated trench that is 6 inches deep and 16 inches wide. The planting depth need not be exact because asparagus roots can accommodate themselves to the soil depth.

Cover the crowns with 2 inches of soil. Then, after the first sprouts grow a few inches tall, fill in the remainder of the trench with soil.

The first year after planting, keep the asparagus bed free of weeds but do not harvest spears. Lightly cultivate in early spring before plants begin growing to help keep weeds in check. Mulching the beds helps, too.

Asparagus is bothered by asparagus beetles. When the stems turn brown in early winter, cut them off at ground level to remove the beetles' overwintering habitat, which helps control the pests.

The second spring after planting, you can harvest spears for about a month when they emerge. Cut them off at ground level when they are about 6 inches long.

In subsequent years, you can cut spears for up to six weeks in spring without weakening the plants.

Clean and fertilize beds every winter while the plants are dormant.

SELECTIONS

For maximum yields, choose all-male, disease-resistant varieties, such as 'Jersey King'. All-male varieties use no energy producing flowers or seeds.

'Mary Washington', a much older strain still found in gardens in which it was planted decades before, produces numerous slender green spears the thickness of a pencil.

A French hybrid called 'Larac' works well if you want to grow pale white asparagus. Its spears turn green if exposed to light but remain creamy white if kept in the dark during the harvest period. You can block out light by placing a temporary black-cloth tunnel over the bed.

A good variety for mild regions (California, the South, and the Northwest) is 'UC 157'.

ASPARAGUS FACTS

Site: Full sun to part shade. Deep, loose, well-drained soil high in organic matter.

Planting: As crowns, 4–6 weeks before average last frost. Spread roots before covering with soil.

Spacing: 5–6 inches deep, 18–24 inches apart.

Care: Water during dry spells. Mulch annually.

Harvest: By snapping off tender young shoots at the base. Do not harvest for the first 2 years after planting, then harvest only for a period of 2–4 weeks. With older plantings, harvest can take place for 5–6 weeks. For highest yields, plant only male cultivars. With all male cultivars, light harvest can begin the year after planting.

Storage: Best flavor is right after harvest, but spears will last in the refrigerator for several days with stems in water.

Peculiarities: Asparagus beetles and weeds are the main challenges. Plant disease resistant cultivars.

BASIL
Ocimum basilicum

'Spicy Globe' basil has a naturally neat growth habit. Here, it's paired with eggplant.

ABOUT BASIL

Although properly classified as an herb, many gardeners grow basil plants in their vegetable gardens. Locate a few plants near the entryway to your garden to fill the air with a delicious aroma as you brush by.

In addition to using basil to flavor tomatoes, green beans, squash, and other vegetables, many gardeners regard basil as a companion plant to these vegetables because

Whether green or bronzy red, basil's fragrant foliage quickly perfumes the summer garden if you gently swish your hand through the leaves. Harvest basil by pinching off the leaf tips. Regular picking keeps the plants full and bushy looking.

their flavors combine so well.

GROWING BASIL

Basil is a warm-season annual. Seed your first crop indoors six to eight weeks before your last frost date. Two weeks after the last frost, when the soil temperature rises to around 70° F, transplant the seedlings in a garden location with full sun and rich, well-drained soil.

Harvest basil leaves as you need them by pinching the growing tips. Pinching off the tops of young plants encourages bushiness. The leafy nodes farther down the stems will quickly develop into new growing tips.

Plants usually stop producing new leaves after flowers appear. Pinch off the green flower spikes as they emerge to encourage continued leaf production, or allow your plants to flower and use the spikes to flavor vinegars. To ensure a continuous supply of basil, start a second crop in early summer.

Basil is susceptible to slugs. It is also easily damaged by light frost. Before the first frost, gather all leaves remaining on a plant and preserve them by freezing, drying, or pureeing into pesto (a paste of basil, garlic, and oil).

SELECTIONS

Basil varieties vary in their flavor, leaf size, and color. 'Minette', 'Minimum', and 'Piccolo' are excellent for garnishes as are 'Fino Verde' and 'Spicy Globe', which grow into tight mounds that work especially well in containers.

"Sweet" basils have larger leaves and are good choices for making pesto. You can also wrap them around fillings. Strains with purple leaves, such as 'Opal', bring interesting visual contrast to gardens and the table and make beautiful ruby- or garnet-colored vinegar.

Scented basils come in a variety of fragrances and flavors. Lemon basil carries a mild citrus accent, while cinnamon basil is spicy. 'Siam Queen' has a moderate licorice undertone.

BASIL FACTS

Site: Full sun. Plentiful water. Well-drained, rich soil.
Planting: Start seed indoors 6–8 weeks before last frost. Set out transplants after danger of frost has passed. Direct seed in midsummer for a second crop.
Spacing: 8–12 inches.
Harvest: Individual leaves. Pinch out flower stems as they appear.
Peculiarities: Occasionally troubled by snails and flea beetles. Sensitive to frost.

Pinch the green flower buds from basil plants as soon as you see them. If allowed to flower, basil stops producing new leaves and the plants decline.

BEANS
Phaseolus vulgaris

ABOUT BEANS

Indulge your sense of adventure by growing different types of beans in your garden. All beans are fast-growing plants that produce flowers in white, purple, and other colors followed by seed-bearing pods. They need full sun and well-drained soil and, except for favas, are warm-weather crops, easily damaged by frost. Bean seeds germinate best in soil temperatures above 60° F.

With the help of soil-borne bacteria, beans are able to take nitrogen from the air and store it in nodules on their roots until it's needed to fuel strong growth. (This process is called nitrogen fixation.) To encourage fixation, dampen the seeds, dust them with inoculant powder, and plant them in warm soil. Avoid using high-nitrogen fertilizers around beans. It can prevent fixation.

Never work around wet bean plants. That spreads diseases.

BUSH BEAN FACTS

Site: Full sun. Part shade reduces yields. Well-drained soil of average fertility, consistent moisture.
Planting: By seed, after danger of frost has passed.
Spacing: 1 inch deep, 2–3 inches apart in rows 18–24 inches apart. Thin to 4–6 inch spacing.
Care: Do not use nitrogen fertilizers.
Harvest: Daily for maximum tenderness. Pick filet beans when pods are ⅛-inch thick or less, snap beans when pods are full sized but seeds small, shell beans when seeds are full sized but not hardened. Let dried beans dry on the plant. Harvest whole plant, then continue drying until beans feel hard. Remove from pods, store in airtight jar. Days to harvest: Varies from 40 (early snaps) to 100 ('Red Kidney').
Peculiarities: Mexican bean beetles, aphids, mildew, bean mosaic virus, anthracnose, rust. Very frost-sensitive. To stop disease spread, do not work among wet plants.

BUSH BEANS

Bush beans grow into knee-high bushes that usually produce edible pods within 60 days after sowing. After the last frost has passed, plant seeds 2 inches apart and 1 inch deep in

Filet beans such as 'Maxibel' have slender pods. They are a true delicacy among snap bean varieties.

full sun and well-drained soil. Thin seedlings to 6 inches apart when they have at least three large leaves. When growing bush beans in small beds or containers, you can space plants as close as 4 inches apart if they get plenty of sun and air circulation.

Once bush beans start producing, you'll get several quick crops in two to three weeks; so make several small sowings three weeks apart. Or, better yet, fill your garden with an assortment of different types of bush beans.

Bush snap beans may have round or flat pods that vary in color from green to yellow to purple (which turn green when cooked). The green-podded 'Provider' is a dependable variety, but there are many others.

Slender-podded French filet beans produce comparatively light crops and are a delight to eat. The petite plants are ideal for growing in small spaces. Pick filet beans daily to ensure tender pods and good flavor.

Another type of bush bean, called horticultural, October, or shell beans, can be harvested as green snap beans when pods are young. Or you can allow them to ripen until seeds become plump and pods feel leathery to the touch. The beans reach their peak flavor before they begin to actually dry. Many varieties grow quite well in northern gardens. If your summers are hot, make them a feature of your late summer and fall gardens. To store horticultural beans, cook, then freeze them.

Dry shell beans grow like other bush beans but have tough, stringy, bitter-tasting pods. Red-kidney, pinto, and black beans are of this type. Allow dry beans to ripen on the plants until the pods turn brown and the plants begin to die. To harvest, pull up plants and

Bush snap beans, such as 'Jade', are easy to grow and provide several pickings over two to three weeks.

PEST WATCH
MEXICAN BEAN BEETLE

The leading pest of garden beans is a mustard-brown beetle with black spots.

Starting in early summer, the adults lay clusters of 40 to 60 bright yellow eggs on the undersides of bean leaves. The eggs hatch into yellow larvae, which rasp away leaf tissue from the undersides. When bean leaves show numerous pale patches, bean beetle larvae often are the cause.

Any garden pesticide labeled for use on beans will kill the beetles if applied to both sides of the leaves. The best natural approach is to handpick the eggs and larvae and use a neem-based insecticide for heavy infestations.

dry them for a week or so in a hot place before cracking open the pods. Spread beans in a single layer on cookie sheets and warm them for 20 minutes in a 175° F oven to kill any pests that might be lurking in them. Store dried beans in an airtight container.

All bush snap beans exhaust themselves after producing two or three heavy pickings and are best pulled up and composted when flowering and pod-setting subside. When bush beans flower well but don't produce many beans, the problem may be heat stress.

Shell beans include red and white October beans as well as pinto, white, red, and black beans.

Temperatures above 90° F can inhibit fertilization.

POLE BEANS

Large pods, full-bodied flavor, and a long season of production are hallmarks of pole beans. Pods come in as many shapes and colors as bush beans, but unlike the latter, the plants grow as vines, which should be trained on a trellis. The trellis can be made from any material: string, wire, thin wooden stakes, or slats.

Plant seeds 8 inches apart. Because pole beans quickly grow into large, heavy plants, install your trellis at the same time as you plant and sow the seeds.

Most pole beans produce their first pods about 60 days after sowing and continue to bear for several weeks. To keep plants productive for a long time, promptly pick young pods before they develop large seeds. If some pods do overripen, harvest them to use as fresh shell beans, discarding the tough shells.

Spraying plants with a kelp solution every three weeks or a light application of blood meal or sidedressing with compost can help produce bumper crops. Follow label directions.

Where the growing season is long, aging pole beans often become seriously weakened by pests and diseases. Remove ragged plants from the garden. In warm regions, you may be able to plant again in late summer for good-quality beans in fall.

For pole beans with deep green pods and a long harvest, try 'Kentucky Blue'. 'Kentucky Wonder' has a fleshy, tender pod that is good fresh or dried.

Scarlet runner beans are easily confused with pole beans, but they are actually a different species, *Phaseolus coccineus*. They produce a profusion of beautiful red blossoms, but the pods are edible only when they are young.

Runner beans often stop blooming in hot weather and are best adapted to climates with cool summers. Scarlet runner has beautiful red flowers, which are attractive to both hummingbirds and children.

Provide a sturdy trellis for long-vined beans. They will wind around wood poles, wire fencing, or heavy string woven between posts and wire. Scarlet runner beans (above) produce pretty red flowers and green pods that are edible only when young. Traditional pole beans produce thick, flavorful pods.

POLE BEAN FACTS

Site: Same as bush beans.
Planting: At base of sturdy bamboo, wooden, or other 5–8-foot poles.
Spacing: 2–3 inches apart or place several seeds at each pole.
Harvest: Same as bush beans.
Peculiarities: Same as bush beans.

BEANS
continued

LIMA BEANS

One great quality of lima beans (*Phaseolus lunatus*) is the ability to tolerate heat, humidity, and challenges from pests and diseases.

Fast-maturing bush limas such as 'Jackson Wonder' will grow in northern gardens, but other limas are most productive in areas with long, hot summers. Limas require warm weather, so plant them in early summer, when the soil temperature is above 75° F.

Sow seeds of bush varieties 3 inches apart. Pole varieties are vigorous plants that require 6-inch spacing and a sturdy trellis.

For buttery flavor, harvest limas when the beans inside the pods are plump but still glossy. When the beans reach this stage of maturity, the pods change from dark green to pale, light green, and the beans become much easier to remove from their pods. Lima beans will keep in the refrigerator for up to a week; they can be frozen or preserved as dry beans.

Lima beans have thick, leathery pods that few insects can penetrate. Because they tolerate heat, you can plant them later than other types of beans. Pole-type varieties grow best in hot climates, but bush varieties often produce good crops during the peak of summer in northern areas.

FAVA BEANS

Fava beans are an ancient legume with a high protein content. Unlike other beans, favas (*Vicia faba*) require cool weather and are hardy to between 10° and 20° F. Plants are large and upright, growing up to 5 feet tall.

Plant fava beans in fall in climates with mild winters or in spring where summers are cool. They usually need at least three months to produce, but take longer when grown over the winter. Favas are tremendous nitrogen fixers and may be used as a cover crop.

Bean sizes vary. Large-seeded strains such as 'Broad Windsor' usually have the best flavor. When mature, the beans are as large as a quarter. To cook as a fresh shell bean, harvest the pods while they are still green. You also can let pods dry and use favas as dry beans.

Some people of Mediterranean descent are strongly allergic to fava beans.

ASPARAGUS BEANS

Also known as yard-long beans, asparagus beans (*Vigna unguiculata*) are vigorous vines closely related to field peas. Asparagus beans grow best in warm climates. They have glossy

LIMA, ASPARAGUS, AND FAVA FACTS

Site: Asparagus beans have the same site needs as bush beans. Limas need warmer weather; favas require a long, cool season.
Planting: By seed, after danger of frost.
Spacing: Limas: same as bush beans; asparagus beans: 1–2 inches deep, 1 inch apart in rows 4 feet apart, thin to 6 to 12 inches; favas: 1–2 inches deep, 1 inch apart in rows 2–3 feet apart. Thin to 6–12 inches.
Harvest: Same as bush beans.
Peculiarities: Limas and asparagus beans have same pests as bush beans; favas are bothered by aphids, thrips, and mites.

leaves and develop purple pea-like pocketbook flowers. The twining stems may grow up to 10 feet long. The pods are quite long, too, often reaching 30 inches. Plant them in late spring, after soil has warmed to 75° F, spacing seeds 8 inches apart. Provide a tepee-type trellis at least 6 feet tall, or train them up a high chain-link fence.

Asparagus beans can tolerate high heat as long as they receive at least 1 inch of water (rain or irrigation) each week. Harvest pods while they are young and green. Asparagus beans cook and eat like snap beans.

The long thin pods of asparagus beans make a good summer substitute for regular snap beans in hot, humid climates.

BEETS
Beta vulgaris

Colorful beets plump up fast when grown in moist, fertile soil. Grow them twice a year, in spring and fall.

ABOUT BEETS

Valued for both their sweet roots and earthy-tasting greens, beets also bring interesting colors to the vegetable garden. Many varieties have bright red leaf stems and leaf veins.

Beets are a cool-season crop best grown in spring and fall. Let them mature in cool soil for the best color and flavor.

GROWING BEETS

Plant beets in fertile, light-textured soil with a neutral or slightly alkaline pH. If your soil is acidic, work in a cup of lime per 10 square feet of planting space. Keeping pH near 7.0 will help prevent scab, a disease of beets. In any type of soil, enrich the bed or row with a 2-inch layer of well-rotted compost before seeding. Be sure to remove any large stones that may impede root growth.

Beet seeds often germinate sporadically. In any soil, you will get a better stand by sowing seeds in shallow trenches filled with a mixture of compost and vermiculite. Plant seeds ½ inch deep and 1 inch apart. Begin planting two to three weeks before your last spring frost. Keep the soil constantly moist until seedlings appear.

In areas where the summers are cool, you can make additional sowings of beets at three-week intervals. In hot-summer climates, make a first small planting in spring and then larger ones in late summer and early fall. Light frosts do not damage fall-grown beets.

Beet seeds are actually a fruit containing several seeds, so you get a particularly thick stand with one sowing. Gradually thin beets to 4 inches apart. You can eat the leaves of young plants. Carefully remove weeds by hand, and mulch around plants with a 1-inch deep layer of organic matter such as grass clippings or compost.

Keeping the soil moist and cool is key to growing sweet, uniform roots. If hot weather arrives before beet roots begin to swell, cool the roots by piling on more mulch or hilling up loose soil around the plants until it just covers the crowns. Because beets are heavy feeders prone to nutrient deficiencies, it is helpful to drench them with a balanced liquid fertilizer or fish emulsion-kelp solution every two weeks as they grow.

Harvest spring- and summer-grown beets when roots reach full size, which varies with variety. Baby beets develop roots 1 inch in diameter in 50 to 55 days, while most table beets grow to 2 inches in diameter in 60 to 70 days. Fall crops that mature in cool soil will hold in the garden for several weeks or until the weather becomes so cold that the soil begins to freeze. Where winters are mild, some hardy varieties can be left in the garden.

SELECTIONS

Fast-maturing hybrid varieties, such as 'Red Ace,' show extra vigor from germination to maturity and are in hot climates and in soils whose fertility and texture are less than ideal. 'Early Wonder' grows more slowly and is popular for the fine flavor of its greens and roots. 'Golden' produces attractive yellow-fleshed roots with a smooth, tender texture.

In deep, loamy soils, try growing cylindrical beets, such as 'Cylindra' and 'Formona'. 'Chioggia' is an unusual variety with pinkish-red and white rings. 'Detroit Dark Red' is a good all-purpose beet for table use, canning, and good greens. For winter beets in zones 7 and 8, grow extra hardy varieties such as 'Lutz Green' or 'Lutz Winterkeeper'.

BEET FACTS

Site: Full sun to part shade. Light, organic soil free of stones. Consistent moisture. Low to average fertility, pH near 7 or higher.

Planting: Seed, 2–3 weeks before last frost. Succession crop every 3 weeks.

Spacing: ¾-inch deep, 1 inch apart in rows 15 inches apart. Thin to 4 inches.

Care: Sidedress with compost or mulch.

Harvest: Baby beets when roots are just rounding out. Days to harvest: 45–60.

Beets grow just below the soil's surface, so you can easily tell when they are ready to harvest. Pull beets as soon as they mature by firmly grasping the tops and pulling them from the soil.

COLE CROPS
continued

varieties, the root stub left behind after cutting the main head often produces tufts of tender leaves that are delicious cooked.

SELECTIONS: Choose cabbage varieties well adapted to your climate and the season in which they are grown. Your local extension office can supply you with this information. Also try varieties with crinkly savoyed leaves, such as 'Salarite'. Fall varieties known for flavor and hardiness include 'Winterstar' and 'Dynamo'. Others that form miniature heads are ideal for small gardens.

CAULIFLOWER

CAULIFLOWER FACTS

Site: Avoid hot or dry.
Spacing: 18 inches apart in rows 32 inches apart.
Care: Protect from heavy frosts. Fertilize monthly with balanced liquid fertilizer. Blanch head by pulling outer leaves over it and holding in place with twist tie.
Harvest: When head is full and firm. Cut with knife at base. Days to harvest: 55–90.

If you are willing to baby it at every stage, you can grow beautiful cauliflower. It matures faster than other cole crops, but for best quality, the plants must have uninterrupted growth. Plant it in spring and again in early fall.

Start seeds indoors four weeks before the last frost in spring, or 10 weeks before the first frost in fall. Grow seedlings under intense light for three weeks and harden off plants for at least a week before transplanting them to the garden.

When the plants develop their first true leaves, fertilize weekly with a half-strength solution of a balanced liquid fertilizer. Grow cauliflower in fertile soil with a near-neutral pH. Space plants 18 inches apart, and mulch lightly.

As soon as small heads form in the centers of the plants, bend the two inner-most leaves over the heads until they break and tie them in place with a twist-tie or clothespin to blanch the heads. Seven to 10 days later, the heads should be ready to cut. Cauliflower bears only one head per plant.
SELECTIONS: Fast-maturing hybrids, such as 'Snow Crown', are the best

Cauliflower responds to attentive care by developing large, mild-flavored heads. Give the plants plenty of space and baby them along with regular fertilizer and water to encourage non-stop growth. Cauliflower is a summer crop in northern areas. Elsewhere, the best-flavored cauliflower matures in fall when temperatures are cool.

choices for a spring crop; they also perform well in fall. Except in the far North, it's best to grow any cauliflower variety that requires more than 80 days to mature in the fall. Cauliflower varieties that produce colorful heads, such as lime-green 'Alverda' or purple 'Violet Queen', also are most dependable when grown from late summer to fall. 'White Rock' is a self-blanching variety with small heads.

COLLARDS

These fast-growing plants, essentially nonheading cabbages, make few demands on the soil and can tolerate a slightly acidic pH and drought. Collards need to mature in cool weather, which improves their flavor. Plants are hardy to between 10° and 15° F.

Sow seeds in late summer so the plants reach picking size just after your first frost. Sow seeds 1 inch apart and ½ inch deep. When seedlings reach 3 to 4 inches tall, thin them to at least 8 inches apart.

Starting in midfall, after one or two frosts, harvest individual leaves from the top third of the plants when they are slightly larger than your hand. Leave the large basal leaves intact.

COLLARDS FACTS

Site: Tolerates drought but quality is best in moist soil.
Spacing: 12 inches apart in rows 20 inches apart.
Care: Mulch overwinter. Stake tall varieties.
Harvest: Pick individual leaves as needed. Days to harvest: 70–85.

Continue to pick leaves this way through winter. In early spring, gather the small green

Grow collards in the fall; the plants reach full size a few weeks after the first frost.

'Red Russian' kale boasts beautiful color and tolerates both heat and cold.

Around the time of your first frost, fertilize the plants with a balanced liquid fertilizer. Or sidedress them with a 1-inch-deep layer of rotted manure. Keep soil moist through the entire growing season.

Cold weather makes kale extra sweet and crisp. Harvest leaves as you need them throughout winter, taking only three or four leaves from each plant at a time. Pull up overwintered plants in spring.

SELECTIONS: Kale varieties with curly leaves, such as 'Winterbor Hybrid' and 'Siberian', become frillier in cold weather. Among smooth-leafed varieties, 'Red Russian' is popular for its red-veined leaves that turn green after cooking.

Kohlrabi develops so fast that you can grow it easily in both spring and fall. Hardy varieties keep in the garden through the first weeks of winter.

flower buds before they turn yellow. Although not well known in the United States, these succulent buds are a delicacy.

SELECTIONS: For fast growth and winter hardiness, 'Champion' is the best bet. The heirloom variety 'Green Glaze' has leaves that are not waxy, and this makes the plants unattractive to imported cabbageworms and other pests. 'Vates' has large, heavy leaves and is a good variety for areas with mild winters.

KALE

This nutritious green comes in many colors—and all are edible, even ornamental kale sold for your flower garden. However, those with green leaves have the sweetest flavor.

You can grow kale in either spring or fall. The young, tender leaves of spring-planted kale are excellent in salads. However, leaves harvested in warm weather lack the sweet, nutty taste of winter-picked leaves. Kale is tremendously winter hardy and you can grow it through winter in almost any region. Where ice and snow are likely to tear the plants apart, grow them under plastic tunnels.

Sow seeds 1 inch apart and ½ inch deep in fertile soil in late summer, about eight weeks before your first frost. Thin the seedlings to 8 inches apart when they grow to be about 4 inches tall.

KALE FACTS

Spacing: 12 inches apart in rows 18 to 24 inches apart. Or direct seed ½ inch deep, 3 inches apart. Thin to 12 inches.

Harvest: Individual leaves as needed.

KOHLRABI

The oddball of the cabbage family, kohlrabi is a fast-growing plant whose stem swells into a round ball just above the soil line. This is the part you eat. Peeled and eaten either raw or cooked, it has a mild, sweet flavor and a texture similar to that of an apple. Because plants mature quickly, you can grow them in both spring and fall.

Sow seed indoors and transplant seedlings when they have five leaves, or plant seeds in the garden, 2 inches apart in fertile soil with a near-neutral pH. Thin plants to 8 inches apart, and water regularly. Fertilize every two weeks with a balanced liquid fertilizer.

Kohlrabi plants are naturally short and stocky. Harvest them in the spring when the stem swells to the size of a tennis ball. They have the best flavor and texture if plants mature in warm weather.

Fall crops will hold in your garden for several weeks, or in zones 7 to 9, they can last all winter. While exposure to cold temperatures improves the flavor of kohlrabi, heat makes its texture woody.

SELECTIONS: In the spring, grow fast-maturing hybrids such as 'Grand Duke', 'Winner', or purple-skinned 'Rapid'. For fall and winter harvest, try giant varieties such as 'Superschmelzt' and 'Gigant Winter'. 'Early Purple Vienna' has purplish stems.

KOHLRABI FACTS

Site: Best with 60°–70° F temperatures.
Planting: Direct-seed.
Harvest: When stems are 2–3 inches in diameter. Slice off at base. Days to harvest: 40–60.

CARROTS
Daucus carota sativus

To grow a kaleidoscope of carrots such as this, plant 'Royal Chantenay', 'Belgium White', 'Little Finger', and other unusual varieties.

ABOUT CARROTS

LOOKING FOR CANTALOUPE? See page 60.

Fresh garden-grown carrots are remarkably crisp and juicy. They come in different shapes and sizes, and even different colors. All carrots grow best in cool weather. In many areas, crops sown in fall can be harvested through winter.

CARROT FACTS

Site: Full sun. Deep, loose soil free of stones, high in organic matter. Plentiful moisture.

Planting: By seed. In North, sow in spring, 2–3 weeks before last average frost. In South, sow seed midwinter through spring, and midsummer into fall. Tip: Sow with radish seed to make it easier on carrot seedlings.

Spacing: ½ inch deep, ½ inch apart, in rows 12 inches apart. Thin to 3 inches.

Care: Mulch to maintain a consistent supply of moisture.

Harvest: Harvest when carrots are fully colored yet tender. Days to harvest: 50–75 days.

Peculiarities: Carrot rust flies, maggots, blight. Exposed "shoulders" can turn green and bitter; mulching keeps shoulders covered. Roots tend to become twisted and forked in heavy, stony soil.

GROWING CARROTS

For carrots to develop long, straight roots, they require deep, sandy loam soil that is free of stones. If your soil is clay, choose short, stubby varieties.

A slightly acidic soil of moderate fertility is best. Dig a ½-inch layer of compost into the soil before planting, but don't add fertilizer if the soil is reasonably fertile. You can lighten the texture of heavy clay soil by amending it with sand or humus.

You can grow carrots in rows or broadcast the seeds in a raised bed. Plant the seeds thickly, allowing three or four per inch of row because some of the seeds will not germinate. Keep soil constantly moist until seedlings appear. After a month, thin the seedlings to 3 inches apart and lightly mulch them.

You can also mix carrot and radish seeds together. The faster-germinating radishes break through soil that's become crusty, making it easier for the carrots to come through and marking their rows. By the time your carrots start to mature, the radishes will be gone.

Wait until carrots reach full size to harvest them because flavor improves with maturity. However, take care to dig up the plants before they turn woody.

To harvest, loosen the soil outside the row with a digging fork, then pull the roots from the soil. Fresh carrots often do not require peeling; simply scrub them with a soft brush.

Carrots develop forked or misshapen roots that are unusually hairy when grown in very fertile soil or given high-nitrogen fertilizer. Clay soil also can contribute to forking. Cracked roots result when dry conditions are followed by heavy rains.

In some areas, the larvae of carrot rust flies tunnel into roots and leave numerous reddish holes behind. Where this pest is a common problem, apply beneficial nematodes to the soil in late spring, or grow carrots under floating row covers. You can prevent problems from the carrot rust flies as well as blight disease of carrots by rotating the crop to different garden sites each year.

SELECTIONS

Experiment to find the best varieties for your soil. Nantes and Imperator hybrids usually produce well in deep sandy loam. Danvers hybrids tolerate both heavy and sandy soils. 'Ingot' is a sweet Nantes carrot. Imperator types include 'Candy Pack', 'Tendersweet', and 'Imperator 58 Improved.' 'Danvers Half Long' is a sweet, crisp carrot that stores well.

Colorful varieties, such as 'Purple Dragon', bring visual excitement to salads. 'Royal Chantenay' is dark orange and juicy.

In clay soils or containers, try miniature carrots that form either round roots or short, blunt, cylindrical roots. Good miniature varieties include round 'Thumbelina', 'Planet', and 'Minicor'.

Unusual 'Purple Dragon' carrots have red skins over orange interiors. They are beautiful sliced into a salad.

CELERY
Apium graveolens

Blanching celery by binding the stems into a bundle helps to keep the inner ribs light colored and tender.

ABOUT CELERY

Homegrown celery is full of flavor and usually darker green than the bunches you buy at the supermarket. Commercial celery producers grow their crops under exacting conditions that are almost impossible to duplicate in most gardens. So why try? Instead, think of your garden celery crop as a unique vegetable that can only be gathered from a home garden.

CONSIDER CELERIAC

Also known as celery root, celeriac is an easy crop as long as you give it plenty of water. Grow seedlings just as you would celery and harvest the roots when they are at least 2 inches across. In fall, you can hill up a few inches of soil over the roots to store them in the ground through early winter.

GROWING CELERY

Cool weather is best for growing celery, but young seedlings must not be exposed to temperatures below 55° F for more than a week. If they are, the plants will flower and set seed prematurely.

Start seeds indoors 10 weeks before your last spring frost. Sow about 20 seeds in a 6-inch pot, cover it with plastic wrap, and keep it moist and warm until the seeds germinate two weeks later. Thin to four plants per pot when the seedlings show their first true leaf.

Before transplanting seedlings to the garden, enrich the soil with as much compost or rotted manure as you can spare. Harden off the seedlings for a few days, but wait until after the last frost to move them into the garden. Leave at least 8 inches between plants.

As plants grow, water as often as needed to keep the soil constantly moist. Fertilize the plants with a balanced liquid fertilizer every two weeks. Begin harvesting individual stalks when they are about 10 inches tall.

To blanch almost-mature plants, wrap the stems with folded newspaper secured with string or large rubber bands. Then hill up soil around the plants to a depth of 6 inches. Harvest the entire plant three weeks after wrapping the stems.

SELECTIONS

Tall Utah types, such as 'Ventura', grow steadily and mature about 100 days after transplanting. 'Ventura' is a tall crisp celery, widely adapted, with some disease resistance.

An heirloom variety called 'Giant Red' has strongly flavored stalks blushed with red. It is best used as a "cutting celery." In other words, harvest individual stalks to use as flavorings in cooked dishes. 'Golden Self-Blanching' forms compact plants.

CELERY FACTS

Site: Full sun to part shade. Rich soil, high in organic matter. Consistent, plentiful moisture. Tolerates poorly drained soil. Long, cool growing season.

Planting: Sow seeds indoors 10 weeks before average last frost. Set out transplants 2 weeks before last frost.

Spacing: 12 inches apart in rows 18 inches apart.

Care: Liquid fertilizer every 3–4 weeks. For milder taste, blanch 2 weeks before harvest by wrapping stalks with paper, a milk carton, or other material. Do not wrap leaves.

Harvest: Cut off entire head at the base with a sharp knife. In climates with mild winters, allow some inner stems to remain to lengthen harvest. Days to harvest: 80–125 days.

Peculiarities: Rarely troubled by insects, but occasionally succumbs to diseases, including black heart and several blights. Keep plants well fertilized and watered and rotate crops to control.

CHARD
Beta vulgaris cicla

ABOUT CHARD

Beautiful and productive, Swiss chard is an ancient vegetable closely related to spinach and beets. You can cook its crinkled, dark green leaves like spinach or lightly steam just the thick leaf ribs to eat like asparagus. Depending on variety, the leaf ribs may be white, red, or a rainbow of colors. Plants are so pretty, they're a fine ornamental edible to grow among flowers.

Chard tolerates hot weather better than other cooking greens do. Plants are also moderately winter hardy. In zones 7 through 9, chard grows in both summer and winter.

GROWING CHARD

Chard is as versatile as it is colorful. A true all-season green for hot or cool weather, enjoy the crisp tops as braised greens, or simply steam the ribs.

Chard needs rich soil and constant moisture. Before planting it, enrich the soil with a 3- to 4-inch layer of compost or rotted manure. Also, add a dusting of lime if the soil is acidic because chard grows best in soil with a nearly neutral pH. Sow seeds in spring for harvest all summer. In areas with mild winters, plant chard again in late summer.

Soak seeds overnight before planting them ½ inch deep and 1 inch apart. The seeds of

CHARD FACTS

Site: Full sun to part shade. Deep, loose, fertile soil, high in organic matter. Consistent moisture. pH of 7.0 or higher. Cool.
Growing considerations: Sow seeds in spring 2–3 weeks before the average last frost.
Spacing: 1 inch deep, 5–6 inches apart, in rows 18 inches apart. Thin to 9 inches.
Care: As plants age, cut back to about 3–5 inches, and plants will send up new shoots.
Harvest: As needed. Cut individual leaves and stalks at soil level, removing only a stalk or two from each plant. Days to harvest: 50–55 days.
Peculiarities: Aphids, leafminers.

chard are actually a fruit that contains several seeds, so seedlings often appear in clusters.

Thin chard seedlings by nipping out the unwanted plants with small scissors. After you have thinned the row or bed to single plants that stand 2 inches apart, you can start pulling and eating the thinnings until your best plants stand 8 inches apart. When growing multicolored chard, wait until you can see different colors in the leaf ribs to do your final thinning.

Mulch chard plants with grass clippings, shredded leaves, or another organic material that will keep soil from splashing up into the leaf crevices. Fertilize the plants each month with a balanced fertilizer. Chard is occasionally bothered by aphids and leafminers, so keep an eye out for them.

Harvest chard by breaking off two or three outer leaves from each plant. If these leaves are more than 12 inches long, discard them and harvest the next layer of leaves. Young leaves less than 10 inches long usually taste best. Chard has a naturally earthy flavor that becomes milder after the leaves are cooked.

To obtain a large quantity of young leaves in fall, cut back the plants to 3 inches tall in late summer. Delicately flavored new leaves will grow from the centers of the plants.

SELECTIONS

The most popular types of chard develop thick leaf ribs the size of celery stalks. 'Lucullus' and 'Fordhook Giant' have white ribs, while 'Rhubarb', 'Vulcan', 'Ruby Red', and 'Charlotte' have bright red leaf veins. 'Large White Ribs' has smooth, dark green leaves as well as white ribs. The mixture called 'Bright Lights' includes plants with leaf ribs in electric shades of red, yellow, orange, white, and green.

CHINESE CABBAGE
Brassica rapa

Napa-type Chinese cabbage varieties produce heavy heads that are packed with crisp, tender leaves.

ABOUT CHINESE CABBAGE

If you take the flavor of cabbage and combine it with the crispness of lettuce, you have Chinese cabbage. There are two major types. Napa Chinese cabbage grows into tightly wrapped, barrel-shaped cylinders. Bok choy has loose leaves that form a cluster of dark green with thick, crisp white veins. Both grow well in any sunny, well-drained spot.

GROWING CHINESE CABBAGE

You can grow Chinese cabbage in both spring and fall. However, as days become longer and warmer in spring, the plants tend to produce flowering stalks at the expense of leaves.

As long as the plants get plenty of water, bok choy varieties produce delightfully crisp leaves with white stalks and leaf veins.

For the best spring crop, sow seeds in individual containers a month before your area's last frost. Transplant seedlings when they are six weeks old, taking care to disturb the roots as little as possible. Sow fall crops in late summer, spacing seeds 3 inches apart and thinning plants to 12 inches when three true leaves develop.

Water regularly and feed plants with a water-soluble fertilizer every two weeks. Never allow the soil to dry out completely. Fertile soil and regular feedings with a liquid fertilizer also help support steady growth. Cover plants with row covers to keep pests in check. Begin harvest as soon as the heads form.

Mature Chinese cabbage tolerates light frosts and will continue to grow after the weather cools in late fall. When hard freezes threaten, cover the plants with an old blanket. Or harvest and store them in the refrigerator.

SELECTIONS

For a spring crop of napa-type Chinese cabbage, choose bolt-resistant hybrid varieties, such as 'Summer Top' or 'Two Seasons'. Other good spring varieties include 'Blues', 'China Express', and 'Spring A-1'.

Any napa variety should perform well in the fall garden. However, you might want to give 'Jade Pagoda' and 'Summertop Napa' a try.

Among bok choy Chinese cabbages, 'Joi Choi' is fast and dependable. A dwarf variety called 'Mei Qing' is especially well suited to small gardens and containers.

CHINESE CABBAGE FACTS

Site: Full sun to part shade. Fertile, well-drained soil high in organic matter. Consistent moisture. Cool.
Planting: Direct-seed in midsummer in northern regions, early fall in southern areas. Or, start indoors 2–3 weeks before setting out. Can grow as a spring crop, transplanting seedlings 4–5 weeks before average last frost. Plant bolt-resistant varieties in spring.
Spacing: ½ inch deep, 1 inch apart, in rows 18 inches apart. Thin to 12–18 inches.
Harvest: In fall before a hard freeze. Cut off heads; remove outer leaves. Days to harvest: 45–90.
Peculiarities: Flea beetles, aphids, cabbageworms, cabbage maggots, slugs.

PEST WATCH
APHIDS

Tiny sucking insects called aphids feed on Chinese cabbage and other garden crops. Sometimes called plant lice, aphids may be green, brown, or pinkish brown. Those that attack Chinese cabbage are gray. Aphids almost always feed in groups. This activity causes minor damage. The major problem from aphids are the diseases that they transmit as they feed on plants. Control aphids with a dilute solution of insecticidal soap. You also can often dislodge them with a strong spray of water. Floating row covers are another solution. The same measures help to discourage flea beetles, which also are common Chinese cabbage pests.

CORN
Zea mays

ABOUT CORN

CORN FACTS

Site: Full sun. Deep, well-drained, fertile soil. Consistent, plentiful moisture. Long, warm season.

Planting: Sow seeds about a week before average last frost. Plant in blocks, not single rows, for best pollination.

Spacing: 1 inch deep, 3–4 inches apart, in rows 2–3 feet apart. Thin plants to 2–3 feet.

Care: Liquid fertilizer every 3 weeks, or broadcast a dry fertilizer at planting and again when plants are about a foot tall. Keep soil evenly moist.

Harvest: After silks turn brown. Check for ripeness by occasionally sampling an ear until kernels are filled out, tender, and sweet. Days to harvest: 60–95 days.

Storage: For maximum flavor, consume as soon as possible.

Peculiarities: Cutworms, corn borers, corn earworms, leaf blights, smut. Well-known as a "heavy feeder."

Sweet corn harvested fresh from the garden is so delicious that you may find yourself eating it raw.

The sugar content of modern sweet corn—super sweet and sugar-enhanced varieties—is higher than in some fruit, no matter whether the corn variety in question has white, yellow, or bicolor kernels.

Corn requires warm weather and more space than most vegetables, but today's hybrids can be grown close together—provided you are willing to give them plenty of supplemental fertilizer. Still, the minimum size for a successful planting of sweet corn is a sunny spot that is at least 6 feet long and 5 feet wide.

Bicolored sweet corn such as 'Sugar Dots' produces ears with a mixture of tender yellow and white kernels.

GROWING CORN

A tropical crop by nature, sweet corn requires warm, fertile soil with a slightly acid pH between 5.8 and 7. Corn is a notoriously heavy feeder, so enrich the soil with rotted manure or compost along with a balanced fertilizer before planting. Organic fertilizers that are rich in alfalfa or blood meal are suitable for corn, or you can mix inexpensive 10-10-10 fertilizer into the site at the rate of 4 cups per 100 feet of planting row.

Customarily, corn is planted in rows spaced 28 to 36 inches apart. For good pollination, plant it in blocks consisting of at least three or four rows. Sow seeds 1 inch deep or slightly deeper if your soil is sandy. Space them 4 inches apart in the row.

Corn will not germinate properly until the soil temperature has risen to 65° F. For a small early planting, start seeds indoors in individual 2-inch peat pots. Set the seedlings out without disturbing their roots after the last frost. The seedlings should have reached 2 inches tall by then. You can also simply wait until a week after the last frost date to make your first sowing in the garden. To stretch the harvest season, plant a midseason variety when early corn reaches 2 inches tall.

Seedlings are vulnerable to cutworms. Because a cutworm wraps itself around the seedling, some gardeners place a nail next to each seedling to prevent the worm from feeding. You can also wrap a paper collar around the base of the seedlings' stems.

PEST WATCH
CORN EARWORM

Hidden beneath a flawless husk, usually near the tip of the ear, you may encounter one or more pasty-beige caterpillars munching away on sweet corn. These are corn earworms, the larvae of a moth that lays eggs on corn silks.

Upon hatching, corn earworms crawl inside the ear and begin to feed. A few drops of mineral oil or granules of *Bacillus thuringiensis* (Bt) placed in the tips of the green ears can reduce infestations. Early crops tend to have fewer earworms, too. Ears damaged by earworms are still fine for eating.

When plants are 6 inches high, thin them to 12 inches apart. If the variety is one that grows very tall (7 to 10 feet), thin seedlings to 2 feet apart. This is also a good time to remove weeds. Use a hoe between rows and hand-weed around plants.

After thinning and weeding, fertilize corn with a light sprinkling of a high-nitrogen fertilizer. If you are using 10-10-10, apply ½ cup per 10 feet of row and scratch it lightly into the soil surface beside the plants.

In the period from pollination to harvest, corn needs 1 inch of water each week. It's best to use drip irrigation hoses at this time to avoid any interference with pollination. A light mulch of straw, shredded leaves, or other organic material will help retain soil moisture as well as suppress weeds.

POLLINATION

The tassels that emerge from the tops of corn plants shed powdery pollen, which must land on newly emerged silks before kernels can develop. Wind does a good job of distributing the pollen in large plantings more than four rows deep. In small plantings, it is helpful to hand-pollinate sweet corn. As soon as the tassels and silks appear, gently gather pollen from the tassels into an envelop and sprinkle it onto the silks of neighboring plants. This is the best way to ensure that the ears will be well filled with uniform kernels.

To safeguard the flavor of fine sweet corn, it is best to prevent cross-pollination with starchy field corn. Plant the two at least 400 feet apart if there's any chance they may develop tassels at the same time. Supersweet varieties must be isolated from all other types of corn, including regular sweet corn, by at least 400 feet. One way to isolate varieties is to stagger plantings so they mature at two-week intervals.

HARVEST

Sweet corn is usually ready about 24 days after the silks appear. Each plant will produce one or two ears. Begin checking ears when the silks appear dry and brown.

Corn is ripe when the kernels look firm and glossy and milky juice bursts out when you puncture a kernel with your fingernail. Sweet corn has the highest sugar content when harvested in the morning. Depending on variety, the sugar content at harvest is between 5 and 10 percent.

In hot weather, the sugar will quickly begin to convert to starch. However, most modern hybrids hold much of their sugar for up to a week when stored in the refrigerator and for several months when frozen.

To ensure complete pollination in a small planting of sweet corn, sprinkle pollen from the tassels onto green silks as soon as the silks emerge. Repeat daily for a week.

SELECTIONS

In short-summer climates, stick with early-maturing varieties such as 'Sugar Buns' or Ontario-bred 'Earlivee'. These and other early varieties produce tasty yellow ears in 65 to 70 days.

The larger, prettier ears of midseason varieties are well worth an extra two-week wait. Varieties described as "sugar enhanced" have a unique combination of sweetness, creamy texture, and rich corn flavor.

There are dozens of excellent varieties from which to choose, including 'Merlin' (yellow), 'Silver King' (white), 'Silver Queen' (white), and 'Sir Galahad' (bicolor). Supersweet corn varieties have a high sugar content, which some people find too sweet for fresh eating. However, varieties such as 'Illini Xtra Sweet' (yellow) or 'Honey 'n Pearl' (bicolor) are excellent choices for freezing.

PRIMING SEEDS

The high sugar content that makes sweet corn so delicious causes the seeds to appear shrunken. Starchy corn, such as that grown for feed, has plump seeds.

Before shriveled sweet corn seeds can germinate, they must slowly plump up with water. To help them along, toss dry seeds with a few drops of vegetable oil, then soak them in room-temperature water overnight before planting. Germinating corn seeds exposed to temperatures below 55° F will die.

CUCUMBERS
Cucumis sativus

Fast, productive, and easy to grow, cucumbers bridge the salad season from spring greens to summer tomatoes, and carry on into fall. Like beans, there are both bush and vine varieties. The huge selection keeps cucumber-loving gardeners happily busy for a lifetime. Many types are so rare that the only way to sample their quality is to grow them.

Like their distant cousins —zucchinis— cucumbers tend to produce more fruit than most gardeners can readily use. Limit the size of plantings unless you plan on making lots of pickles. Six plants of any type will provide dozens of fruit to eat and share.

With luck, planning, and timely use of season-stretching techniques, most gardeners can grow two or three crops each summer. Make a first planting in spring, a second in early summer, and if you live in the South, a third about 10 weeks before your area's first expected fall frost. When frost is predicted, gather all plants left in the garden, because even a light frost will kill them.

CUCUMBER FACTS

Site: Full sun. Warm, well-drained, organic soil. Plentiful moisture. Long growing season. Can tolerate cooler temperatures and a wider range of soil types than other melons.
Planting: Sow seeds in hills or rows after last frost. In southern areas, plant in midspring and in midsummer for two harvests.
Spacing: 1½ inches deep, 4–6 seeds per hill, or 3–4 feet apart in and between rows. Thin to three plants per hill.
Harvest: As soon as fruits reach full size. Do not allow to become large and seedy, or production will greatly decrease. Days to harvest: 55–70.
Peculiarities: Cucumber beetles, bacterial wilt, anthracnose, mildew, mosaic virus, scab, leaf spot. Grow resistant varieties to prevent diseases. May develop bitter taste in dry sites.

PEST WATCH
STRIPED CUCUMBER BEETLE

These ¼-inch-long, winged, yellow beetles with black stripes on their backs always manage to find cucumber plants. Adults feed on flowers, leaves, and fruit, and the larvae eat cucumber roots.

As they feed, the adults often transmit from one plant to another an incurable disease called bacterial wilt. This disease causes vines to wilt and die within a week.

Row covers are the easiest way to protect plants from striped cucumber beetle damage. Yellow sticky traps also help reduce their populations in the garden.

Any reasonably good soil with a near-neutral pH will support cucumbers. However, the soil should be well-drained.

Cucumbers require warm weather to grow. Direct sow seeds when the soil temperature is above 70° F. At these temperatures, you expect excellent germination. When the seedlings develop their first true leaves, thin the plants to at least 6 inches apart.

Gardeners in areas with short growing seasons can get a head start by starting transplants indoors. Sow the seeds a month before the last frost. Harden seedlings off before setting them out. At the same time, place black plastic or dark-colored compost over the planting site to warm up the soil.

A cucumber trellis saves space, increases light exposure to the plants' leaves, and helps keep long fruit straight and pretty.

Tradition calls for cucumbers to be sown in hills or mounds, but you may also plant them in rows, beds, or containers. Set plants out under tunnels covered with fabric row covers or perforated plastic to protect them from insect pests and late-season cold winds. When the plants begin to flower, remove the covers to allow pollinating insects to enter.

Plant spacing and trellising requirements vary among varieties. Compact, short-vined types need no support, but any cucumber allowed to run over the ground benefits from light mulch to help keep fruit clean.

A simple tepee-type trellis for a trio of plants increases production and saves space as does chain-link fencing. Cucumbers with long fruit, such as Oriental and Armenian varieties, need a sturdy trellis made of string, wire, or polyester net to keep the fruit straight. To train the vines up any type of trellis, tie them in place with soft pieces of cloth or hosiery.

Regular deep watering helps cucumbers to grow quickly. Within six weeks after planting, yellow flowers will begin to appear. After another week, you should see tiny fruit at the base of some of the flowers. Those blossoms are female; the ones on slender stems without fruit are male. Only female flowers set fruit.

CUCUMBER VOCABULARY

Gynoecious: Varieties that produce only female flowers, which tend to set fruit early. Female flowers have a bulge on the blossom stem that looks like a tiny cucumber. Seed companies usually include a few blue-tinted seeds in packets of gynoecious cucumber seeds. These are males, which are necessary for pollination. So be sure that you plant at least one of these blue seeds.

Parthenocarpic: Varieties that produce self-fertile female flowers. If you are growing a parthenocarpic variety under a row cover, there is no need to lift the cover to admit honeybees and other pollinating insects.

Nonbitter cucumbers: Varieties that lack bitter flavor. Their leaves do not develop the chemical compound that stimulates feeding by cucumber beetles.

Burpless cucumbers: Cucumbers with thin, tender skin, which makes them easy to digest without peeling. Also, these cucumbers lack the compound that makes cucumbers bitter and hard to digest.

Disease resistant: Varieties seldom bothered by the many diseases that can attack cucumbers, such as powdery mildew, anthracnose, and mosaic virus.

Cucumbers are prone to a number of diseases including anthracnose, mildew, mosaic virus, leaf spot, scab, and bacterial wilt. Many of these diseases are spread by insects (see box on page 52). To control these diseases, plant resistant varieties and destroy infected plants.

As soon as the fruit begins to swell, make sure that your cucumbers never run short of water. Moist soil enhances fruit quality.

Pick cucumbers young, before the seeds inside mature and harden. Push on the stem with your thumb until the fruit breaks free. Refrigerate the fruit to keep it firm and crisp.

SELECTIONS

The typical 8-inch-long, dark green cucumbers sold at grocery stores are American hybrids. Exemplary varieties for home gardens include slicing cucumbers such as 'Fanfare' and 'Straight Eight'. Both are productive and disease resistant.

Oriental varieties like 'Suyo Long' and 'Orient Express' need a trellis to keep from developing kinks and curls. The fruit is mild flavored and burpless.

The burpless variety 'Sweet Success' combines the flavor and size of Oriental cucumbers with the vigor and productivity of American hybrids. It is self-fertile and can grow under row covers until the fruit ripens.

Bush cucumbers include 'Spacemaster' and 'Salad Bush'. Each has tender 8-inch fruit. The plants are disease resistant.

Flavorful Middle Eastern varieties, such as 'Amira', develop light green-skinned fruit that is best when it reaches 4 to 5 inches long.

Small-fruited pickling cucumbers tend to produce dozens of small fruit all at once. Use them fresh in salads as well as pickling.

Compact pickling varieties, such as 'Bush Baby' and 'Bush Pickle', fit easily into small gardens and containers. 'H-19 Little Leaf' is both parthenocarpic and disease resistant. 'Vert de Massy' is good for tiny, French-style cornichon pickles.

Catalogs also list numerous novelty cucumbers including 'Lemon', 'Apple', and others with light skin. These are as easy to grow as pickling types but usually not as productive.

Oriental cucumbers have long, slender fruit.

American hybrids have straight, blocky shapes.

Pickling cucumbers can be preserved or eaten fresh.

EGGPLANT
Solanum melongena

ABOUT EGGPLANT

A perennial in tropical climates, eggplant grows as an annual in the vegetable garden. It tolerates high heat and humidity extremely well, but in cool climates, it will barely grow. Where nights are consistently cooler than 65° F, the plants may fail to set fruit altogether.

In warm climates where eggplant is laden with glossy fruit and starry, lavender flowers, the plants are pretty, too.

EGGPLANT FACTS

Site: Full sun. Well-drained, fertile soil, high in organic matter. Tolerates a broad range of soils and moderate moisture.
Planting: Start transplants 10–12 weeks before average last frost. Wait 2 weeks after last frost before transplanting.
Spacing: 18–24 inches apart in rows 30 inches apart.
Care: Stake plants that have a heavy fruit set. Mulch. Does well with black plastic mulch. Needs two or more months with night-time temperatures of 70–80° F.
Harvest: Cut fruit when full, firm, tender and glossy. Days to harvest from transplanting: 65–80.
Peculiarities: Colorado potato beetles, cutworms, flea beetles.

Harvest eggplant fruit young, while the skins are still glossy. Cut them from the plants with the green sepals attached.

GROWING EGGPLANT

All eggplant varieties grow well in areas where the summers are long. Buy seedlings in late spring or start seeds indoors 8 to 10 weeks before your last frost. Except in warm climates, there is little reason to start them any earlier because eggplant will not grow outdoors until the weather is warm.

After sowing, place the seed flats or containers in a warm, well-lit place. Eggplant seed germinates best at 85° F.

Eggplant is frost sensitive so wait one to two weeks after the average date of the last frost to transplant seedlings. The best site is one with slightly acid soil (a pH between 5.6 and 6.8) that is rich in organic matter. Set plants 20 inches apart and enrich each planting hole with at least a gallon of good compost or rotted manure. After transplanting, cover plants with milk-carton cloches or plastic tunnels for two weeks to protect them from late cold spells.

Where summers are cool, grow eggplant under tunnels covered with sheets of perforated white or clear plastic or beneath a loose row cover, which also protects plants from flea beetles.

Oriental eggplant varieties that produce long, cylindrical fruit are good choices for areas with a short growing season as are small-fruited varieties.

You also can grow eggplants in large black plastic pots, which help keep roots warm. Grow the potted plants on a bench. Raising plants protects them from early-summer flea beetles, usually sustaining only light feeding.

Fruit is ripe when it turns glossy. Cut it from the plants, taking a short stub of stem along with the cap. Young fruit has the best flavor and texture. If you discover well-formed seeds within an eggplant, this is a sure sign that the fruit is overripe.

SELECTIONS

Choose varieties based on your climate. In northern areas, fast-maturing hybrids that produce small- to medium-sized fruit are best. Rewarding choices include 'Neon', which has medium-sized cylindrical fruit with pinkish-purple skin. Various elongated, Oriental varieties are also good. These include pink-skinned 'Bride', 'Ichiban', and 'Orient Express', both of which have purple skin.

In small gardens and containers, try baby eggplant varieties, such as 'Bambino'. As long as warm conditions prevail, these varieties will produce their first fruit about 70 days after transplanting.

Because the fruit does not freeze well, plant only as much as you think you will eat fresh. Eggplant is self-fertile, so you need to grow only one plant of any variety. 'Black Beauty' is a high-yielding, widely adapted purple variety. In warm climates, large-fruited varieties such as 'Black Bell' will produce about five fruit per plant. You can easily harvest a dozen or more fruit from 'Dusky' and other small-fruited varieties. In warmer regions, green-fruited varieties such as 'Louisiana Light Green' often survive mild winters and produce for two or three years.

FENNEL
Foeniculum vulgare azoricum

Make room for Florence fennel in a fall garden. Cool, moist soil results in large, tender bulbs.

ABOUT FENNEL

Fennel is an Italian vegetable also known as finocchio or Florence fennel. The leaves have the classic fragrance and flavor of the herb fennel, but this vegetable's main attraction is its crisp aboveground bulb. Made up of flattened stalks similar to those of celery, the bulb has a nutty, slightly aniselike flavor, which becomes sweeter when cooked. Although unfamiliar to many American gardeners, fennel's flavor is delicious.

GROWING FENNEL

Fennel is a cool-season vegetable that tends to bolt prematurely if you plant it in spring. In northern areas, you can plant fennel two to three weeks before the last frost, but it is ideal for sowing in summer for harvest in mid to late fall. In much of the southern United States, August is the best month for planting.

Seeds germinate well in hot soil if you keep the soil consistently moist. Sow seeds 1 inch apart and ½ inch deep in rich soil with a near-neutral pH. You can also start plants indoors in containers, setting them out when they develop a tuft of ferny leaves.

Whether you start fennel by seeds or transplants, it is important for it to be actively growing as soon as the weather begins to cool in early fall. The seedlings will grow slowly at first, then take off when cool weather arrives.

The garden site for Florence fennel should have full sun and well-drained soil. Fennel tolerates dry soil, as long as it contains plenty of organic matter.

Thin or transplant seedlings to 8 inches apart, then mulch lightly with grass clippings, compost, or straw to keep the soil cool and moist. Because fennel grows into a slender, upright plant, it does a poor job of shading out nearby weeds. Pull weeds that sprout within a few inches of your fennel by hand.

To help the plants grow and reach harvestable size quickly, drench them every two weeks with a balanced liquid fertilizer. When the bulbs begin to swell, add more mulch to blanch them, which keeps them extra tender.

Harvest plants as you need them in the kitchen by pulling them up, roots and all. Use a sharp knife to cut off the roots and leafy tops, keeping only the tender bulb. Remove the outermost two or three stems from the bulb. These are tough and stringy.

Fennel plants can withstand light frosts, but they are usually damaged by temperatures below 26° F. The day before your first hard freeze, gather up the bulbs remaining in the garden and store them in the refrigerator.

SELECTIONS

When buying fennel, take care to ensure you bring home the right plant. Herb fennel (*Foeniculum vulgare dulce*) does not produce a bulb, even though it is closely related to Florence fennel. You will find Florence fennel clearly listed in seed catalogs under that name.

The variety 'Zefa Fino' is widely available, but a few seed companies offer other selections. 'Herald' is good for early planting. It resists bolting.

FENNEL FACTS

Site: Full sun. Well-drained soil, high in organic matter. Adaptable to broad range of soil and climatic conditions.
Planting: Direct sow 2–3 weeks before average last frost. Can continue sowing seeds through the summer. Generally planted in late summer in southern regions.
Spacing: ¼ inch deep, 1 inch apart, in rows 2 feet apart.
Harvest: Leafy stalks for flavoring soups, salads. Cut at soil level, when base of plant is about 3–4 inches in diameter. Days to harvest: 65–90.
Peculiarities: No major disease or insect pests. Plants may require staking.

LOOKING FOR ENDIVE?
See page 79.

The tender stems inside a fennel bulb have a sweet, nutty flavor unlike that of any other vegetable. Discard the tough outside stems before slicing and cooking the tasty hearts.

GARLIC
Allium sativum

While waiting for the plants to mature, snip off tender, young leaves from garlic plants for cooking.

GARLIC FACTS

Site: Full sun. Well-drained, fertile soil. Slightly dry.

Planting: By individual cloves split from a garlic bulb. Leaving papery husk on the cloves, set cloves with tips up. Plant in October to early November in northern regions, November through January in the South. Northern gardeners who miss a fall planting may succeed with an early-spring planting, if soil is loose and well-prepared.

Spacing: 2 inches deep, 6 inches apart; elephant garlic requires slightly wider spacing.

Care: Mulch plantings. To grow larger bulbs, remove woody flower stalks as they appear.

Harvest: In summer when at least half of the leaves have begun to yellow and the "necks" are still soft. Cure bulbs by drying in a warm, well-ventilated spot for several days.

Storage: Cut off tops after curing. Store in a cool, dry place. Many varieties will keep for 6–8 months.

Peculiarities: Bulbs may rot in heavy, wet soils. Otherwise, no serious pests or diseases.

You can braid the tops of softneck garlic and hang the bulbs in a dry place until you need them for cooking. In fall, replant only the largest outer cloves from the bulbs.

ABOUT GARLIC

Whether you begin with garlic purchased from the grocery or buy special varieties from a seed catalog, a single clove planted in fall will develop into a round, many-cloved bulb by the following summer.

However, garlic often changes its growth pattern from one climate to another. To fairly evaluate a specific variety, save a bulb or two from your garden each year and replant its cloves. Judge the plant's performance after at least two crops.

GROWING GARLIC

There are three types of garlic: stiffneck, softneck, and elephant. Stiffneck types are the most cold hardy and are dependable in zones 3 and 4. They're made up of a few large, mild-flavored cloves around a stiff central stem.

The large bulbs sold in groceries are usually softneck types. They are mild tasting and easy to peel. These are the ones whose tops you can braid before storing. Most softneck garlics are hardy to zone 4, but some survive only to zone 7. In warm areas, these tender varieties can hold onto some green growth all winter. When buying starts by mail, be sure to pay attention to hardiness zone listings.

Elephant garlic produces a few extremely large, mild flavored cloves. In areas colder than zone 7, plant it the first thing in spring. It is the least cold hardy of the three types.

The best time to plant garlic is in mid to late fall. Break off the large outer cloves from a bulb and plant them pointed end up in rich, well-drained soil. Use the small inner cloves for cooking. Set the cloves 1½ inches deep and 6 inches apart. In cold winter areas, mulch heavily after the ground freezes to limit soil heaving from repeated freezing and thawing. Rake off the mulch in early spring. When top growth starts to appear, make sure plants receive at least an inch of water per week.

As the soil warms, plants quickly grow 2 and 4 feet tall. For the largest bulbs, cut off the woody flowering stalks when they emerge from the centers of the plants. If you allow stiffneck strains to flower, they will produce small edible top-set cloves, which may be eaten or replanted, however, their bulbs will be smaller than normal.

When the foliage starts to yellow in mid- to late summer, gently dig the plants and allow the bulbs to cure in a warm, dry place. You can braid the leaves of softneck types, but stiffneck and elephant garlic store best hanging in mesh bags in a dry place.

SELECTIONS

'Italian Late' (softneck) tastes great and stores well. 'German Extra Hardy' resists heaving.

HORSERADISH
Armoracia rusticana

Horseradish is a low-maintenance perennial vegetable that persists and spreads in the garden for many years.

ABOUT HORSERADISH

A tough perennial grown for its pungent roots, horseradish is virtually indestructible. Gardeners should note that this plant is moderately aggressive. Locate it in a corner of the garden where you will not accidentally dig and spread root pieces, which readily develop into new plants. It takes only a few plants to provide plenty of horseradish for the average family.

GROWING HORSERADISH

Grow horseradish from root cuttings in a fertile, well-drained spot. Lay the 6-inch-long root pieces diagonally in a 6-inch-deep trench so that the top end (the one with the largest cut) is almost at the soil surface. Plant the pieces 12 inches apart in a row or in a circle to form a round clump. By early summer, the roots will send up large green leaves, which persist until fall.

To help plants develop thick, smooth roots, you can pull the soil away from the topmost part of the plant. Then with a sharp knife, nick off as many of the slender side roots as you can reach. These side roots sprout from the main root and divert resources from the main root. Afterwards, the soil.

To harvest horseradish, dig up plants in fall or spring. Use a sharp knife to cut away the thick primary root. Replant roots that are slightly thicker than a pencil and discard small stringy roots.

Once a large colony of horseradish becomes well established, you can harvest roots anytime you want by digging plants from the outside of the clump. Should errant plants appear where they are not wanted, promptly dig them up and allow them to dry in the sun so they don't reroot and spread to other areas of the garden.

Horseradish roots contain a pungent oil similar to that found in hot peppers. It can burn your skin and make your eyes water. Work with the roots in a well-ventilated area—outdoors whenever possible—and wear rubber gloves when peeling or grating the roots. To keep freshly grated horseradish root from turning brown, mix lemon juice or vinegar into the gratings.

SELECTIONS

Horseradish is not sold by variety name. You can plant roots purchased at the grocery store or you can buy starter roots through seed catalogs.

GOOD NEIGHBORS

Jerusalem artichoke (page 76) is another vigorous root crop that is best planted at the garden's edge to keep it from getting out of hand. It grows well beside horseradish because horseradish tolerates the filtered shade from a taller neighbor. You can dig and replant both crops anytime from fall until spring.

HORSERADISH FACTS

Site: Full sun. Well-drained soil. Tolerant of a range of sites and of neglect. Avoid sites that you cultivate, which may spread the roots throughout the garden.
Planting: Root cuttings in spring. Any live piece of root will "take."
Spacing: 24 inches apart.
Harvest: Dig roots in the fall; they are extremely pungent.
Peculiarities: No major insect or disease problems.

LOOKING FOR JERUSALEM ARTICHOKE?
See page 76.

LOOKING FOR KALE OR KOHLRABI?
See page 45.

Wear rubber gloves when working with horseradish roots. They contain an oil similar to that found in hot peppers and can burn your hands.

LETTUCE
Lactuca sativa

LETTUCE FACTS

Site: Full sun to part shade. Well-drained, cool, loose soil. Plentiful moisture. Adaptable to many growing conditions, but (60°–70° F) temperatures are best.
Planting: By seed in spring as soon as the soil can be worked. Broadcast in a patch or sow in a row. Plant every 3 weeks for succession crops.
Spacing: ⅛ inch deep, 1 inch apart in rows 12 inches apart.
Care: Keep soil moist. Mulch. Lightly spray every 2 weeks with liquid fertilizer such as seaweed or fish emulsion to push harvest.
Harvest: For heading types, remove entire head with a knife at the base. Alternatively, and for other types, remove outer leaves, allowing the inner ones to continue growing, for cut-and-come-again harvest. Days to harvest: 45–85.
Peculiarities: Slugs, tip burn in hot weather.

'Sierra' is a beautiful "French crisp" variety. It forms a barrel-shaped head packed with sweet crunchy leaves.

ABOUT LETTUCE

LOOKING FOR LEEKS?
See page 65.

Grow different kinds of leaf lettuce for a variety of colors and textures in your salads. Lettuce becomes bitter when the plants begin to flower.

Lettuce generally is a cool-season crop, but by choosing cold-hardy and heat-tolerant varieties and using special cultural techniques, you can grow it almost all year. In addition to head lettuces, such as iceberg, several types of leaf lettuce are available, each with varying shapes and textures of leaves. Among these varieties are romaine or cos lettuces, Boston or butterheads, and loose-leaf lettuces.

GROWING LETTUCE

Lettuce is 90 percent water and has shallow roots, so the soil in which it grows must hold moisture well. In sandy soil, dig a 2-inch layer of compost into the bed before setting out plants or sowing seeds. Enrich all soil types with a light application of a balanced, slow-release fertilizer before planting.

Because lettuce grows so fast and typically is eaten raw rather than stored, it is better to make a succession of small plantings, than one single large sowing. Plant only 1 or 2 square feet of garden space at a time. A good strategy is to make three plantings in spring and two more in fall.

To get a jump on spring, start seeds indoors about four weeks before the last frost. Always use fresh seed when planting lettuce because seeds more than two years old may not germinate.

Sow seeds in small containers or cell packs. After germination, place seedlings under strong lights to encourage stocky growth. Move them outdoors into a cold frame when they are a month old. Or transplant them to the garden under the protection of a cloche or cold frame.

When the danger of hard frost has passed, transplant the seedlings into the garden, spacing them 6 inches apart. At the same time as you set out seedlings, make a small sowing in a finely cultivated bed, spacing seeds 1 inch apart in all directions. Lightly cover the seeds with compost, peat moss, or other material that will not form a crust.

With constant moisture, the seeds should germinate quickly and seedlings should be ready to thin in two weeks. First, thin plants to 2 inches apart. Two weeks later, thin the plants again to 4 to 6 inches apart. (Add the thinnings to your salad.)

'Buttercrunch' lettuce has the vigor of 'Bibb' types, with a delicate texture similar to that of butterhead varieties.

Some of the best varieties for growing through winter are butterheads. The heads form in early spring.

If you prefer, you can harvest tightly spaced baby lettuce by cutting handfuls of leaves just above the plants' crowns with a sharp knife. Lettuce spaced too closely and harvested in this way will quickly produce new leaves, but plants will remain small. For large heads, thin plants to 8 to 12 inches apart.

Where the summers are warm, make subsequent sowings where the plants will receive partial shade. One strategy to is grow a small nursery bed of heat-tolerant varieties and dig and transplant individual plants to spots where they will receive afternoon shade from tomatoes or other large vegetables. As long as you lift seedlings from beneath, keep soil packed around their roots, and water the transplants regularly, they are quite willing to move to new locations.

Should lettuce plants grow slowly or show yellowing of the outer leaves, fertilize them every 10 days with a water-soluble fertilizer mixed at half strength.

Pull up plants as soon as the main stem begins to lengthen, spiral upward and form flowers. This is bolting. When lettuce bolts, the plants grow tall. New leaves are small, have a dull finish, and taste bitter. Spring-planted lettuce usually bolts in early summer.

In late summer, start an early fall crop of seedlings indoors. Most lettuce varieties will not germinate in hot soil, but they will grow beautifully when started indoors and set out as soon as nights become cool. Begin direct-sowing cold-tolerant lettuce varieties at the same time you set out fall seedlings.

The hardiest lettuce varieties will grow under plastic tunnels throughout the winter. When they are protected from ice and snow beneath a tunnel, winter lettuce can survive in the garden at temperatures to 10° F (or lower). When the days lengthen again early in the spring, these plants will start to explode with new growth.

Don't be surprised if your winter lettuce has a slightly fibrous texture. The new leaves that form in spring will be much more tender and palatable.

SELECTIONS

One of the great joys of growing lettuce is experimenting with the many varieties available. Leaf lettuce varieties are easy to grow and include numerous selections that vary in size, color, and texture. 'Green Ice' is light green and crispy, while 'Red Sails' develops large crinkly leaves edged with bright red. 'Black-Seeded Simpson' is an early lettuce with extra-large leaves. Colorful red-leafed varieties are as easy to grow as those with vibrant green leaves.

For a summer crop, try heat-tolerant 'Salad Bowl' or 'Oakleaf' in the filtered shade beneath tomatoes or corn. Many seed companies now sell mixtures of several leaf-lettuce varieties of varying shapes and colors. These are ideal for cutting as baby lettuce.

If crispness is a priority, you will like the thick white veins that make up the leaves of butterhead lettuces, such as 'Buttercrunch' and 'Bibb'.

Hardy varieties that can be overwintered as immature seedlings include delicate butterheads such as 'Arctic King' and 'North Pole', as well as a unique variety called 'Winter Density', which looks like a cross between a butterhead and a romaine.

With the exception of 'Summertime' and a few other varieties that develop small heads, iceberg lettuce grows slowly and needs more cool weather than most climates have to offer. When subjected to the heat of early summer, many iceberg types bolt before their heads reach full size. Easy alternatives are Batavian- or French-crisp lettuce varieties, such as 'Sierra' or 'Nevada'. The inner leaves are as sweet and crisp as those found within round iceberg heads, but the plants are much easier to grow.

Sturdy romaine, or cos, lettuce is a great choice for a fall crop because it tastes best when it matures in cool weather. Varieties such as green 'Plato' and bronze 'Rouge d'Hiver' also are quite cold hardy. When sown in early fall, these will hold in the garden under plastic tunnels well into winter. Other good varieties to look for include 'Parris Island Cos', 'Parris White Cos', 'Little Caesar', and 'Jericho'.

With all winter lettuce varieties, a plastic tunnel or cold frame will enhance the plants' winter hardiness and reduce the possibility that their soft leaves will be injured by rain or hail.

Romaine varieties such as 'Rosalita' taste best when they mature in cool fall weather and get plenty of water.

LOOKING FOR MÂCHE AND MESCLUN?
See page 78.

MELONS
Cucumis melo

MELON FACTS

Site: Full sun. Warm, well-drained soil, high in organic matter. Consistent, plentiful moisture. Long growing season.
Planting: Direct sow seed 1–2 weeks after average last frost. Or, start transplants in peat pots 3 weeks before you set them out.
Spacing: 6 seeds per hill, hills 4–6 feet apart; or seeds 1 foot apart in rows 5 feet apart. Can plant at closer spacings if trellised. Thin plants so that 2–3 remain per hill.
Care: Melons grow well with plastic mulch; remove plastic when hot weather arrives. Otherwise, use organic mulch. To prevent insect damage, set developing fruits on pots or pieces of wood. For trellised melons, support fruits with a sling made from netting, fabric, or panty hose.
Harvest: Generally, fruit is ripe when the stem separates from fruit with only slight pressure; color may deepen and yellow; blossom end may soften; noticeable sweet aroma. 70–100 days from transplant to harvest.
Peculiarities: Cucumber beetles, mildew, wilt. Sensitive to frost.

The rich, sweet flavor of muskmelons is matched by their high nutritional value. They are packed with vitamin A.

ABOUT MELONS

LOOKING FOR WATERMELON?
See page 88.

Honeydews are one of the three melons suitable for growing in home vegetable gardens.

Three types of melons are well-suited to home gardens: true cantaloupes, muskmelons and winter melons.

■ True cantaloupes have a warty, ribbed rind and sweet, bright orange flesh. Technically, a true cantaloupe is a French or Charentais melon. The cantaloupe you buy at the grocery is actually a muskmelon.

■ Muskmelons have netted, yellowish rinds and orange flesh.

■ Winter melons vary in their appearance. For example, casabas have a wrinkled, golden rind and white flesh; honeydews, a smooth rind and green flesh; crenshaws, a yellow rind and salmon pink flesh. Persian melons are round, have a netted rind and thick orange flesh, and are larger than muskmelons.

All melons are hybrids of the species *Cucumis melo*, and they all have the same growing needs. They are warm-season plants, closely related to cucumbers. Their vines run along the ground, and plants have both male and female flowers. Only the female flowers form melons, and they must be pollinated by insects to do so.

Depending on the variety of the melon and the health of the plant, you can expect to harvest from three to five melons from each plant.

GROWING MELONS

Because melons produce male and female flowers that require cross-pollination, grow at least five plants of any variety to be sure that there is plenty of pollen for bees and other insects to spread among the blossoms.

The plants require a site with full sun and well-drained soil that is high in organic matter. They grow best in hot weather and need plenty of water while vines are running.

Vines usually grow at least 10 feet long, and it is important that every leaf receives full exposure to bright sun. In rows, space plants 3 feet apart. You also can grow melons in hills spaced 5 feet apart, with two to three plants in each hill. Either way, you will need a space 15 feet wide and 20 feet long for six plants.

Sow seeds directly in fertile soil when the soil temperature is at least 70° F. Or start seeds indoors in 3- or 4-inch pots and set out seedlings one week after the average date of your area's last frost.

Weeds can be an aggravating problem because you can't always get to them among the vines. Covering the soil between rows with black plastic or paper mulch at planting time is an excellent weed-prevention strategy.

Several insects, including spotted and striped cucumber beetles, can cripple unprotected plants. The simplest way to prevent insect injury is to cover seedlings with floating row cover as soon as they are planted and mulched. Make sure the cover fits loosely and leave some fabric to accommodate growing vines. Instead of burying all the edges, keep one side secured with boards so you can easily lift the cover to check on plants and let in pollinators.

Crenshaw melons have a sweet mellow flavor and soft texture. The rambling vines produce large oval fruits.

If plants grow slowly or their leaves turn yellow, fertilize them with a balanced liquid or granular fertilizer soon after the vines begin to run.

The first flowers that appear will probably be males, which cannot set fruit. A mix of male and female flowers usually opens about a week after the first flowers appear. When this occurs, remove the row covers for two or three days to allow pollinating insects access to the flowers. Some harmful insects will enter the planting during this time. Before putting the row cover back on, thoroughly spray the plants with water to get the insects moving. Handpick squash bugs and cucumber beetles that crawl to the top of the leaves. As further insurance against damage by insects, treat the plants with a neem-based insecticide before replacing the row covers.

Melons need water (1 inch per week) while they are vining, yet the flavor of the fruit is best when you allow the soil to become somewhat dry as the melons reach full size and ripen. Slight wilting of the leaves is normal in the middle of a hot summer day, but do not allow the soil to become so dry that the leaves remain wilted into the evening.

HARVESTING

Use all of your senses to tell when melons are fully ripe. The first test is to examine them with your eyes. Many muskmelons develop a textured surface on the outside of the melon, called netting, which turns buff-brown as the fruit ripens. Honeydews with smooth rinds change colors, too, from creamy green to ivory-yellow.

Also check the point where the stem joins the fruit. Many melons begin to separate from the stem as they ripen, evidenced by small cracks at the stem end of the fruit. Gently pushing on the stem will cause the fruit to "slip" or break free. Sometimes the leaf closest to the melon also turns yellow as the fruit ripens.

With muskmelons, you can usually detect a distinct fruity aroma by sniffing the blossom end of a ripe fruit.

Stored at room temperature, melons will keep up to two weeks after harvest.

SELECTIONS

Among muskmelons, both the 'Earlisweet' and the 'Earliqueen' varieties mature quickly and produce 3- to 4-pound fruit on disease-resistant vines. Another hybrid, 'Pulsar', matures two weeks later and has larger melons. 'Pulsar' develops a strong fragrance as the melons ripen, and the fruit tends to separate from the stem when it's ready to pick. 'Earligold' has large fruit and resists mildew. 'Ananas' grows well in southern regions.

Charentais melons produce small, 2-pound fruit with spicy yet sweet orange flesh. Two excellent varieties that mature in about 80 days are 'Alienor' and 'Savor'. They do not slip from the vine when ripe, so check the leaves closest to the melon instead. 'Pancha' forms small, intensely sweet melons.

Good winter melons include 'Earlidew', a honeydew hybrid that forms 2- to 3-pound melons. 'Passport' produces 3- to 6-pound fruit with a high sugar content and complex flavor reminiscent of tropical fruit. 'Marygold' is a sweet early casaba.

PEST WATCH
SPOTTED CUCUMBER BEETLE

These bright yellow beetles with black spots on their backs feed on melon leaves, blossoms, and fruit. However, they do the worst damage by infecting plants with a disease called bacterial wilt.

Infected plants gradually wilt and die over a period of one to two weeks, and there is no way to restore their health.

The best way to protect plants is to grow them under lightweight floating row covers. Alternatively, place yellow sticky traps among your vines to snare the beetles. Once you start finding beetles in the traps, treat plants weekly with an insecticide labeled for use on cucumber family crops.

Protect ripening fruit from insects and rot by setting it on stones, bricks, or squares of cardboard.

MUSTARD

Brassica juncea, B. rapa

MUSTARD FACTS

Site: Full sun to part shade. Well-drained, fertile soil, high in organic matter. Consistent, moisture. Widely adapted, but cool temperatures best.

Planting: By seed. Sow every 2 weeks for continuous harvest. Generally planted in late summer in southern regions; harvest in the fall.

Spacing: ½ inch deep, 1 inch apart, in rows 6–8 inches apart. Thin to 6 inches.

Care: Soil should remain moist. Tolerates light frost.

Harvest: Harvest leaves cut-and-come-again fashion. Days to harvest: 40–80.

Peculiarities: Flea beetles.

Oriental mustards such as 'Tatsoi' have a mild flavor and are pretty enough to grow among flowers.

ABOUT MUSTARD

Mustard is one of those plant-and-stand-back crops. The seeds will germinate almost as soon as they hit the ground, and the leaves come on so fast and strong that mustard is sometimes used as a short-term cover crop.

Processed mustard, sold as a condiment, is made from seeds of an entirely different species than leaf mustard. However, if you let leaf mustard mature and develop seeds, you can blend the seeds with honey and vinegar to make a zesty salad dressing. And if you allow a spring crop of mustard to shed its seeds in the garden, you likely will be rewarded with a number of volunteer seedlings in fall.

In addition to planting mustard in the vegetable garden, you can use it as a foliage plant among flowers. Oriental and red-leaf varieties make fine background plants for your fall marigolds, chrysanthemums, and pansies.

GROWING MUSTARD

All of the mustards are cool season crops for spring or fall. They grow in almost any soil and require only regular watering.

Plant seeds in early spring while the soil is still cool. For a fall crop, sow the seeds about seven weeks before the first frost. Space seeds 1 inch apart and sow them ½ inch deep. Thin plants to 8 inches apart when they have more than three leaves.

To harvest mustard, cut individual leaves as you need them or pull up entire plants. Unlike other greens whose leaves taste best when harvested young, mustard's flavor improves as the plants mature. If you like pungent greens, you can chop up the young leaves and combine them with lettuce in salads.

SELECTIONS

American varieties of mustard grow into large, 2-foot-tall plants. They produce bumper crops of crisp, green leaves with curled edges. These mustards, including 'Green Wave' and 'Southern Giant', have a peppery flavor that becomes tamer and more succulent after you cook it.

Japanese strains of mustard with red leaves, which include 'Osaka Purple' and 'Red Giant', have a bite similar to American mustards. Their red leaves are a popular accent for accompanying flowers in the garden. 'Osaka Purple' reaches only about 12 inches tall, while 'Red Giant' often grows to 18 inches in height.

Oriental mustards are distinctive. They have a milder flavor than other mustards, and the plants develop into symmetrical round mounds which are quite beautiful in the garden.

One variety, 'Tah Tsai' (also spelled Tatsoi), is sometimes called spinach mustard. It has glossy, dark green, spoon-shaped leaves, which develop into a circular ground-hugging rosette. 'Tah Tsai' tends to bolt when grown in spring, but it's an outstanding fall crop.

Other oriental mustards include 'Mizuna,' with long, narrow, feathery leaves that are mild enough to enjoy raw in salads. Or you can use them in stir-fried dishes. It does well in both spring and fall. 'Miiki Giant' has crinkly, pungent, purple leaves. It is also cold hardy, lasting in the garden well into winter.

OKRA
Abelmoschus esculentus

Okra pods mature quickly in hot weather. Frequent harvesting encourages plants to develop new flowers and pods.

ABOUT OKRA

One look at okra's big yellow blossoms will tell you that it is a member of the hibiscus family. Unlike hibiscus, though, the immature seedpods, which form after the blossoms shrivel, are edible. Originally from North Africa, okra requires warm weather for good growth. In areas where it grows well, a single sowing in early summer will produce tender young pods nonstop until frost.

GROWING OKRA

Plants do best in a somewhat dry soil. In warm climates, avoid planting okra in rich soil or overapplying high-nitrogen fertilizers. Overfertilized plants produce huge leaves and few pods.

Okra is susceptible to root-knot nematode, so don't plant it in infested soil. Other pests of okra include aphids, flea beetles, and virus wilt.

Okra seeds have a hard seed coat and germinate faster if you soak them in water overnight before planting. In areas where the growing season is short or cool, start seeds indoors in 2-inch peat pots in late spring. Keep the containers warm to encourage germination. Thin to one seedling per pot after sprouts appear.

To raise garden soil temperatures a few degrees before planting, cover the bed or row with black plastic mulch. Transplant the seedlings into holes cut in the plastic as soon as the soil has warmed, but at least three weeks after the last frost. Handle the brittle seedlings as gently as possible and do not disturb their roots. Space plants 12 inches apart in the garden.

In warm climates, direct-sow okra seeds in early summer in areas left vacant by cool-season crops, such as lettuce, potatoes, or peas. Plant soaked seeds 3 inches apart and 1 inch deep. When the seedlings are 6 inches tall, thin them to 18 inches apart. Okra's large leaves shade the soil and discourage weeds so much that mulching usually is not necessary.

Prune plants in late summer to encourage growth of lateral branches, which will produce new flowers and pods. Cut the main stem back by one-third its height, then water plants well to promote strong, new growth.

HARVESTING

Use a sharp knife or pruning shears to harvest tender young pods before they reach 5 inches long. Cut a stub of stem with the pod. As you harvest young pods, also cut off tough overgrown pods and compost them. Once plants produce mature seeds, they often stop flowering.

Many people develop a contact dermatitis from touching the prickly hairs on plants and pods. As a precaution, wear gloves and a long-sleeved shirt when working around okra.

SELECTIONS

Older okra varieties often do not produce well in northern gardens, but most modern varieties make a good crop if established by early summer. Early dwarf varieties, such as 'Annie Oakley' or 'Lee', fit nicely into small gardens and are the best choices for cool summers.

In warm climates, 'Cajun Delight' is so productive that you may need fewer than a dozen plants to meet your family's needs. Red-podded 'Burgundy' is an interesting, edible ornamental. Its pods turn green when cooked. If you are sensitive to the prickly hairs, try 'Clemson Spineless', which has no hairs.

OKRA FACTS

Site: Full sun. Well-drained, dry, slightly alkaline soil. Warm temperatures.

Planting: Direct seed after danger of frost has passed. In southern regions, make successive sowings from late April through mid-August. Do not overwater.

Spacing: ½ inch deep, 1 inch apart, in rows 24 inches apart. Thin to 15 inches.

Harvest: Harvest pods when 4 inches long. Days to harvest: 50–60.

Peculiarities: Sports irritating hairs that bother some gardeners.

ONIONS AND LEEKS

Allium spp.

ABOUT ONIONS

The onion family includes a vast assortment of pungent, highly flavorful vegetables, as well as some spectacular varieties of flowering bulbs for ornamental gardens. Most types of onion grow in any garden, while leeks are an outstanding garden crop in areas where summers stay cool.

In addition to the familiar bulb onions, there are also perpetual—or perennial—onions. These include leeks, chives, shallots, nest onions, and bunching onions (also called green onions or scallions).

Nest onions are like shallots. They form clusters of small bulbs at their base. To keep perpetual onions going from year to year, plant divisions in fall or spring.

ONION FACTS

Site: Full sun. Well-drained, soil high in organic matter, neutral pH. Consistent, plentiful moisture.

Planting: By seed, transplants or sets (tiny bulbs). Sow seed indoors 4–6 weeks before setting out. Transplant seedlings, plant sets, or direct sow seed 3–4 weeks before average last frost in north or in the fall in south.

Spacing: Transplants: 1 inch deep, 3 inches apart. Sets: 2½ inches deep, 1 inch apart. Direct-sown seed: ¼ inch deep, ½ inch apart. Thin to 4 inches. 15-inch row spacing.

Care: Blanch scallion types by wrapping base with soil. Control weeds.

Harvest: Scallions: about 8 weeks after planting or when 12 inches tall. Bulbs: when tops begin to fall over. Cure by drying in a dry area with good air circulation. Immediately harvest bulb onions which begin to bolt.

Storage: Trim leaves so that 1 inch remains above bulb when outer skins feel papery and dry. Store at around 40° F. Days to harvest varies by type and variety, from little pearl onions (55) to 'Walla Walla' (up to 300).

Peculiarities: Thrips, onion maggots, soil-borne diseases. Move all onions to a new site each year to avoid problems.

Before storing bulb onions, lay them out to cure for several days.

BULB ONIONS

Bulb onions are heavy feeders requiring rich, well-drained soil with a near-neutral pH, between 6 and 7. In acid soil, onion flavor is more pungent. Enrich the garden site with rotted manure or compost before planting and mix in a standard application of a balanced fertilizer.

You can plant onions from seeds, plants, or small dormant bulbs called sets. Seeds need about 10 weeks to grow to transplanting size. Most gardeners save time by starting with purchased plants or sets, which are widely available in spring.

Plant sets or seedlings 3 inches apart (and 3 inches deep for sets). A month or so later, harvest every other plant for use as scallions.

Weed bulb onions often and use a light mulch of grass clippings or straw to help keep soil moist. Drench plants monthly with a balanced water-soluble fertilizer. Clip off any flower stalks that appear, because flowering reduces the size and quality of the bulbs.

When the bulbs swell and the tops of the plants begin to yellow, knock over the tops to stop bulbs from growing and to allow them to ripen. After a week, pull up the bulbs and cure them in a warm, dry place.

SELECTIONS

In the South, where summer days are only 14 hours long, choose short-day varieties, such as 'Yellow Granex', which mature in early summer. Other short-day varieties are 'Valley Sweet', which is resistant to pinkroot onion disease, 'Red Creole', a pungent onion, and 'New Mexico White Granno', a large, mild white onion. Northern gardeners can grow numerous long-day varieties, which begin to form bulbs after they are exposed to 15- to 16-hour-long days. 'Walla Walla' and other sweet-Spanish types have the mildest flavor. 'Mambo' is a good storage onion with a strong flavor. Other long-day varieties are superior storage onions. For the small pearl onions, try 'Red Baby' and 'Snow Baby'.

SHALLOTS AND NEST ONIONS

Shallots and nest onions make excellent mild-flavored crops. Instead of producing one large bulb, each splits into a cluster of 3 to 10 small teardrop-shaped onions. Save the largest ones for replanting.

In the South, plant shallots and nest onions in the fall in fertile, well-drained soil. Where winters are frigid, plant the bulbs in early spring. Keep rows free of weeds and fertilize the plants monthly from late spring onward.

Shallots split into a cluster of mild-flavored bulbs as they mature. Dry the bulblets well before storing them.

Harvest nest onions when tops die back. Store in a cool, dry place until replanting time; don't leave them in the ground when dormant or you will invite problems with onion root maggots and soil-borne diseases.

Specialty seed companies sell dormant sets of many heirloom varieties, which usually are shipped in the fall or early spring.

BUNCHING ONIONS AND CHIVES

Instead of forming bulbs, chives and bunching onions multiply by dividing into upright clumps. No garden should be without these easy-to-grow plants. However, scallions do best in cool, moist conditions.

Start with seeds or plants set out in spring in any sunny well-drained spot. Clip leaves from chives as you need them in the kitchen, but don't harvest bunching onions until fall. Both types often "die back" or go dormant in midsummer. When the weather cools, they again produce new tops.

In the fall, harvest bunching onions as you need them by digging them up and pulling them apart. Replant some in a new spot, and they will again form bunches in spring. In cold-winter regions, plant divisions in pots. Keep them indoors in a cool, well-lighted spot, then replant them in the garden early the next spring.

When properly handled, bunching scallion varieties such as 'Evergreen White Bunching', 'Deep Purple', or 'Evergreen Hardy White' will produce tender scallions almost all year.

Propagate chives by digging them in fall. Cut each clump into sections and replant the sections in a new site. In areas where chives are not hardy, plant some divisions into 8-inch pots. Bring one pot in to keep on a sunny windowsill for use through winter and leave the rest outdoors until just after the first hard freeze. Store the dormant potted chives in a cool basement or garage for the winter. Replant them outdoors in spring.

Chives produce edible purple flowers in spring and tangy leaves all summer. Divide and replant clumps when new growth appears in spring.

LEEKS

Leeks grow much like bulb onions. They thrive in cool weather and may be grown from fall through spring in mild-winter areas. In the North, start the seeds indoors in late winter. Set out the seedlings in spring in a rich soil, spacing plants 10 inches apart.

Mulch leeks with at least 4 inches of rich organic material to keep the roots cool and constantly moist. Apply a balanced liquid fertilizer monthly.

You can begin harvesting leeks when the shanks grow more than an inch thick. Where summers are cool and moist, leeks sometimes grow into giant plants 4 feet tall with long white shanks that may be 3 inches thick.

Leeks benefit from a long, cool growing season. Tuck extra soil and mulch around the base of the plants to increase the length and thickness of the white shanks.

LEEK FACTS

Site: Same as for onions.
Planting: Sow seed indoors 8 weeks before average last frost date. Transplant around the last frost date. Or direct seed 4 weeks before the average last frost.
Spacing: 4 inches deep, 4 inches apart in rows 20 inches apart. Direct seed ½ inch deep, 1 inch apart, rows 20 inches apart. Thin to 4 inches.
Care: To blanch, mound soil around stems as leeks grow. Alternatively, place a portion of a cardboard paper-towel roll around the lower part of the stem. Plants respond well to mulching.
Harvest: Pull when base of the stem is about an inch around.
Days to harvest: 70–120.
Peculiarities: Trouble-free.

PARSLEY
Petroselinum crispum

Compact, curly parsley makes a nice edging for gardens, or try growing it as an ornamental among flowers or larger vegetables.

ABOUT PARSLEY

Whether densely curled or flat, parsley's pretty green leaves bring flavor and color to food. Hardy, as well, parsley makes a great ornamental plant to slip among flowers or other vegetables. Though best known for its leaves, some varieties also develop thick edible roots that can be harvested like carrots at the end of the season.

PARSLEY FACTS

Site: Full sun to part shade. Well-drained, fertile soil high in organic matter. Plentiful, consistent moisture. Cool weather.
Planting: Sow seed indoors 10 weeks before average last frost. Transplant outside around the average last frost date. Direct seed in fall. Parsley is a biennial. It may re-seed in the garden.
Spacing: 6 inches apart.
Harvest: Individual leaves as needed.
Peculiarities: Attracts parsley worm, the larvae of the swallowtail butterfly. Seed may be slow to germinate. To speed germination, soak it for several hours before planting.

LOOKING FOR PARSNIPS?
See page 74.

Flat-leaf parsley has more flavor than curly types. After drying, its flavor becomes even more concentrated.

GROWING PARSLEY

Parsley can withstand both summer heat and winter cold. It is a biennial so it usually doesn't flower until its second spring after sowing. However, exposure to cold weather triggers flowering in biennials, and a late cold snap can chill parsley and force it to flower its first year in the garden.

For a continuous supply of leaves, sow a few seeds every spring and fall. Patience is required with parsley seed because it often takes three weeks to sprout. Seeds germinate best when soil temperatures range between 50° and 70° F. Soak the seed in water overnight before planting. Then sow it ½ inch deep and ½ inch apart in fertile, neutral soil. When parsley seedlings develop their first true leaves, thin them to 10 inches apart.

You can also start seed indoors in pots, keeping soil constantly moist until seedlings appear. Set out container-grown seedlings without disturbing the roots. When plants grow to 2 inches tall, mulch between them to keep the soil cool and moist.

Harvest parsley by pinching off stems as you need them. Healthy plants usually survive winter even though their tops may be killed back to the ground. The next spring, the year-old plants produce a fresh crop of leaves, then send up large yellow umbels—umbrella-like clusters—of flowers, signaling the end of the planting. If space permits, allow the flowers to remain in the garden for a few weeks.

They attract tiny wasps and other beneficial insects. You may be disturbed by the appearance of huge yellow and black striped worms feeding on your parsley. These are larvae of the beautiful swallowtail butterfly. In fact, parsley is a choice plant for butterfly gardens, but if the larvae are troublesome, you can use a row cover to protect your crop or pick the larvae off by hand. With a continuous crop, you may have enough for yourself and the butterflies.

SELECTIONS

Curly types of parsley are usually dwarf plants that grow less than 12 inches tall. They have a mild flavor and must be mulched to keep soil from accumulating in the leaf crevices. Flat-leaf or Italian parsley has a stronger flavor, and the plants may grow to 18 inches tall. A third type of parsley, called Hamburg or parsnip-rooted parsley, produces leaves with flavor similar to flat parsley and long, white edible roots. When sown in spring, you can harvest the roots in the fall. Cool soil improves their flavor.

Whether you start plants in spring or fall, parsley will flower after exposure to chilly weather.

PEANUT
Arachis hypogaea

Peanuts are ready to harvest when the shells are stiff and seeds inside have dark red skins.

ABOUT PEANUTS

Originally from South America, peanuts were long known as groundnuts because the "nuts" —or, more appropriately, seeds—form under the ground like potatoes. Nearly tropical in temperament, peanuts require at least 120 days of warm weather to make a good crop. With consistent warmth, a single plant can produce more than 50 peanuts.

GROWING PEANUTS

Peanuts do best in light, sandy soil that is high in organic matter, but they will grow in clay if it is amended to improve drainage. Incorporate a light application of a balanced fertilizer into the soil before planting. Because peanuts are legumes, they help provide for their own nutritional needs by fixing nitrogen.

In the North, start seeds indoors in peat pots four weeks before the last frost. Transplant the seedlings when the soil warms to 60° to 70° F. In the South, after the soil has warmed in late spring, plant seeds—whole peanuts—6 inches apart. Make sure the seeds come from a nursery and not from the grocery. When planting, keep the reddish seed coat intact. This thin skin acts as a barrier to disease while the seeds are germinating.

Plants grow up to 3 feet across, so space them in single rows at least 24 inches wide. Thin plants to 15 inches apart in the row about a month after planting. Hoe regularly to control weeds and to keep soil loose and slightly hilled up in an 18-inch-wide circle around the base of each plant.

In midsummer, numerous short stems will emerge from the centers of the plants, each one topped with a little yellow flower. After the flowers fade, these stems become pegs, which gradually bend over and "plant" themselves. At the end of each peg, a peanut forms. Keep soil beneath plants loose and moist during this process, then lightly mulch after the pegs have penetrated the soil.

When the leaves begin to yellow in late summer or early fall, dig a sample plant to check for ripeness. When mature, most of the peanuts should have stiff shells and their seed coats should be reddish brown rather than pink. If the nuts are not ripe, wait 10 days before sampling another plant.

Harvest peanuts when the soil is dry. After loosening the outside of the row with a digging fork, pull up plants by grabbing the tops with both hands. Shake off the soil. In clay soil, it helps to quickly rinse the roots with a strong spray of water.

Lay harvested plants out to dry in warm sun for about 10 days. While the peanuts are curing, you can pick off small immature seeds, wash them well, and boil them in salted water before eating. Remove mature nuts from the plants when thoroughly dry. Store them in a cool, dry, well-ventilated place.

SELECTIONS

There are Spanish-type peanuts, such as 'Valencia', which produce slender pods packed with several small nuts, and jumbo Virginia peanuts, which produce one or two large nuts in each pod. If you live where peanuts are grown commercially, many varieties are available. One to try is 'Jumbo Virginia', which produces high yields of large peanuts on compact plants.

Unlike any other vegetable, peanuts produce seeds on "pegs," which burrow into the ground after the flowers are fertilized.

PEAS
Pisum sativum, Vigna unguiculata

ABOUT PEAS

Treasures of the spring garden, shell (English), snow, and snap peas collectively make up the group known as garden peas. These are cool-season crops. Where the growing season offers at least three months of warm, 80° F days, semi-tropical field peas thrive.

GARDEN PEA FACTS

Site: Full sun to part shade. Well-drained soil of average fertility, high in organic matter. Cool, damp.

Planting: North: Sow seed in spring as soon as soil can be worked. Plant again in early fall, although fall crops may not be as reliable if hot weather persists. South: Plant in fall and late winter.

Spacing: 2 inches deep, 3 inches apart, in rows 18 inches apart.

Care: Do not use high nitrogen fertilizers. Trellis vining types. Keep soil moist.

Harvest: Shell or snow peas: when pods fill out. Snap peas: when peas are full, yet still tender. Dry peas: let harden on the plant; harvest the whole plant, allow to dry, then remove peas from pods. Days to harvest: 55–75.

Peculiarities: Heavy watering or rain during flowering can interfere with pollination. Bothered by rabbits and aphids.

Consider inoculating pea seeds before planting them in a new garden. The bacteria in the inoculant helps plants fix nitrogen.

GROWING GARDEN PEAS

Young garden peas are cold hardy and not damaged by heavy frost. Sow them as soon as the soil can be worked up to a month before your last spring frost is expected. An early start is important because peas must flower and set fruit before temperatures reach 80° F. Once hot weather arrives, no new pods will form. However, pods already set will continue growing.

One strategy for stretching the harvest season is to plant on the same day two or three varieties that mature at different times.

In areas where nights cool to 50° to 60° F in August, you can plant peas in July for fall harvest. However, in most areas, growing peas in the fall is tricky. Warm nights slow the plants' growth well into fall, and subfreezing weather damages nearly mature plants. To increase your chances of success with fall peas, grow only dwarf varieties that mature quickly.

Grow peas in rich, moist, well-drained soil where they have not been planted for at least two years. Pea roots host a persistent soil-borne fungus that builds up quickly and causes root rot.

Before planting peas, lightly fertilize the space with a balanced fertilizer. Install a trellis down the middle of the row to help support the vines. Tall varieties grow best on a 5-foot trellis made of chicken wire, string, or polyester netting. You can support compact varieties by pushing twiggy branches into the

Grow shell peas for the sweet, succulent seeds inside the pods.

soil down the center of the row. Peas also grow well on a chain-link fence. Young plants may need help to find their support at first.

To save space, plant peas in double rows, leaving 10 inches between rows. Sow seeds 2 inches apart. Thin seedlings to 4 inches apart when they are 2 inches tall.

After the plants are a few inches tall, they will take nitrogen from the air and store it in nodules on their roots until it is needed. This is a process called nitrogen fixation.

When planting peas in new garden soil, you might want to treat the seeds with an inoculant to ensure fixation. This inexpensive powder contains the bacteria that help peas fix nitrogen and places it in the soil right next to their roots. Place a tablespoon of inoculant in a jar with soaked or dampened pea seeds. Shake the jar gently to coat seeds with the powder.

Both the pods and the seeds of snap peas are edible.

Harvest shell peas when the pods are still glossy and the raw peas inside taste sweet and tender. Pick snow peas when the peas just begin to swell into small lumps. Snap peas taste best when the pods are plump and the peas inside are young and tender.

Refrigerate garden peas as soon as you pick them. Special varieties grown for drying may be left on plants until pods become dull and

waxy and begin to dry to a tan color.

Snow peas produce thin, crispy pods with tiny, sweet peas inside.

SELECTIONS

Only the seeds inside the pods of shell peas are edible. Modern varieties such as 'Maestro' are resistant to a virus of peas and powdery mildew, serious problems in the Northwest and areas of the upper Midwest. (Rodents also can be a problem for peas.)

In areas where the pea virus does not pose a threat, try older varieties famous for their rich pea flavor, including 'Green Arrow' and 'Thomas Laxton'. Leafless varieties, which develop stems and tendrils but few leaves, are highly resistant to powdery mildew, so they are ideal for planting in late summer when this disease is most prevalent.

Peas hold onto trellises with curly tendrils. You can support them with sticks, string, polyester netting, or wire mesh.

You can eat the pods and the seeds of snow peas and snap peas. Among snow peas, 'Oregon Giant' is disease resistant, and its large pods are sweet and crisp, as are 'Ho Lohn Dow' and 'Oregon Sugar Pod II'. Snap peas are delicious fresh or frozen and are tremendously productive. 'Sugar Snap' grows to 5 feet tall. Dwarf varieties need only a short trellis. 'Alaska' and other starchy peas are best for drying.

GROWING FIELD PEAS

These legumes go by many names, including black- or pink-eyed peas, crowders, and cream peas. Each name defines a certain type of field pea whose large species group is also called cowpeas or Southern peas.

Field peas are warm-weather crops that thrive on heat too intense for most vegetables. They grow best in the South and Southwest. Plant them from early to midsummer in space left vacant by cool-season crops.

Sow the seed 4 inches apart. Thin seedlings to 10 inches apart when they are 3 inches tall. Field peas have few pests. They benefit from regular watering during hot, dry weather. For fresh eating, harvest the peas when the texture of the pods changes from firm to slightly leathery. The peas inside should be plump and glossy.

SELECTIONS

In areas where field peas are popular garden crops, the best variety choices are at local feed and seed stores. In most areas, pink-eyed varieties are most productive. Pods turn purple when the peas are ready to pick.

Crowder peas are strong nitrogen fixers, ideal for growing in poor soil. Some varieties develop small peas—sometimes called lady peas or cream peas. These are delectable to eat but can be tedious to shell.

'Mississippi Silver' (left) and 'Pinkeye Purple Hull' (right) are among the most popular and productive field pea varieties.

Black-eyed and other field peas thrive in hot weather.

COWPEAS FACTS

Site: See asparagus bean on page 40. Preferred in the South over limas and snap beans because of their resistance to heat, insects.
Spacing: Sow seeds 1–2 inches deep, 1 inch apart, 2–3 feet between rows. Thin plants to 6–12 inches within row.
Harvest: Pick pods as you would green shell beans or leave them on the plant as dry peas. Days to harvest: 55–75.
Peculiarities: Susceptible to cold weather injury; typically grown in the southern states.

PEPPERS
Capsicum annuum

PEPPER FACTS

Site: Full sun. Well-drained, light, fertile soil, high in organic matter. Warm.

Planting: By transplants. Sow seed indoors, ¼ inch deep, 8–10 weeks before setting out. Keep flats or peat pots indoors in a warm, sunny location. Transplant 2 weeks after average last frost.

Spacing: 18–24 inches apart in rows 24 inches apart.

Care: Mulch with either organic or plastic materials. Two to three light sprays of a liquid fertilizer such as seaweed or fish emulsion can be beneficial. High nitrogen fertilizers promote vegetative growth instead of fruit production.

Harvest: Remove fruit by cutting when full-sized and either fully colored or still green. Green peppers will turn red (or other colors) as they mature. Use rubber gloves when preparing hot varieties. Days to harvest from transplanting: 60–75.

Peculiarities: Temperamental fruit set if temperatures are too hot or cold. Pests include tarnished plant bug, aphids, sunscald. Blossom end rot is a disorder caused in part by an uneven supply of moisture; mulching helps by keeping soil moisture levels even.

Green peppers become much sweeter when fully ripened. At maturity, they may be red, yellow, orange, or purple.

ABOUT PEPPERS

Growing peppers can be a hobby in itself. With exacting care, plants provide a never-ending stream of fruit which—depending on the variety—may be sweet, spicy, pungent, or hot.

Peppers are tropical perennials that grow best when temperatures range between 65° and 85° F. For them to fully ripen in short-summer areas, gardeners must make use of every warm day. Set out pepper transplants as soon as possible in early spring. Cover them with cloches or tunnels to raise temperatures.

Where summers are hot, peppers often remain barren through summer, then produce dozens of fruit when nights cool in early fall. These peppers won't fully ripen but will provide you with plenty of sweet green peppers.

'Gypsy', a Caribbean hybrid, has the mild flavor of sweet bell peppers but a more elongated shape. As the fruit ripens, it changes from green to orange to red.

GROWING PEPPERS

STARTING SEEDLINGS: Many varieties of pepper transplants are available in spring, or you can start them at home. Sow seed 6 to 10 weeks before the last frost. Seeds germinate best at 75° to 80° F. When watering, use tepid water to keep the temperature up.

Pepper seedlings need intense light, continuous warmth, and room to grow with unrestricted roots. Transplant seedlings to 4-inch pots as soon as they have four leaves. Keep plants indoors under lights or in a warm cold frame until days reach 70° F and nights are above 55° F. Then harden off seedlings for at least a week before setting them out in the garden.

SITE: In the garden, grow peppers in any sunny, well-drained spot rich with organic matter. Peppers benefit from two or three hours of afternoon shade in hot climates.

Dig planting holes 12 inches deep and wide and enrich each hole with a gallon of compost. If soil is sandy or infertile, mix half the normal application rate of a tomato fertilizer into the soil before planting. Tomato fertilizers are low in nitrogen and usually have an analysis of 5-6-5 or 3-5-6. Apply the other half as a side-dressing after the plants set a few fruit. If you apply too much fertilizer peppers grow into large plants with only a few peppers.

TRANSPLANTING: Set out seedlings on a warm, cloudy day, spacing them 18 inches apart. Plant them an inch or so deeper than they grew in their pots because deep planting insulates the plants' roots from temperature changes and helps keep them moist.

Protect the transplants with a cloche. In cool climates, you also can grow peppers under plastic tunnels or inside wire cages wrapped with clear plastic. A mulch of black plastic or black landscape-fabric weed barrier also help the soil stay warm. Where warmth is not an issue, mulch peppers with grass clippings, straw, or any material that maintains soil moisture. Water peppers as often as needed to keep the soil lightly moist at all times.

FRUIT SET: Peppers develop fruit when nighttime temperatures are above 65° F and daytime temperatures below 95° F. Extreme heat or cold leads to failed flowers and no fruit. However, small-fruited peppers often fruit when large bells do not.

In hot climates, large bell peppers set fruit better if temporarily shaded in midsummer. The simplest way to do this is to cover plants with a sheet attached to stakes. Make sure air can circulate under the cloth. The cover also prevents sun scald in bright sunlight.

Peppers are occasionally troubled by tarnished plant bugs and aphids and are susceptible to blossom end rot. Mulching to keep the soil moist will prevent this disease.

HARVEST: You can harvest peppers when they are green, but sweet peppers become much richer and sweet flavored when they fully mature to their ripe color, which may be red, yellow, or orange. When green peppers show a few stripes of color, they will continue to ripen off the plants if kept in a warm 75° F place after harvest. Brittle pepper stems break easily, so cut off fruit with a knife or pruning shears.

The pungency of hot peppers strongly correlates with variety, and warm weather also maximizes their heat. In other words, the same hot pepper that matures in cool, 60° F conditions will not be as sharp as one that ripens in 90° F weather. Harvest hot peppers when they change color or when the seeds inside are hard and fully formed when you open the fruit.

Sweet and hot banana peppers set fruit in weather that makes other kinds of peppers temperamental.

The pungency of hot peppers is rated in terms of Scoville Units (S.U.). Mildly pungent peppers include hybrids with long, tapered fruit and S.U. ratings of less than 3,000 units. These flavorful varieties make great salsa, as reflected in such variety names as 'Garden Salsa', 'Salsa Delight', and 'Sugarchile'.

For roasting and stuffing, grow large poblanos, anaheims, or 'NuMex' chiles with modest pungency ratings of 1,000 to 1,500 S.U. These peppers usually mature in less than 80 days from transplanting, but they don't produce well where nights are extremely cool or warm.

Jalapeños are easy to grow in many climates and are available in both hot and mild forms. 'Senorita' has a low heat rating, while other varieties deliver much more fire with ratings to 10,000 S.U. Slightly hotter serrano peppers have a hot, biting unique flavor that many associate with spicy Mexican food. Cayennes, habaneros, and most Thai peppers are extremely hot and should be handled with care. Their S.U. ratings range from 50,000 to more than 100,000. When cutting hot peppers, wear rubber gloves and keep your hands away from your face and eyes.

SELECTIONS

Sweet peppers include the typical blocky bell peppers and numerous varieties with pods shaped like conical tops, cones, and even bananas. 'Ace' and 'Northstar' are famous for their ripe red fruit in cool northern climates.

Large peppers are best grown where there is plenty of warmth in late summer. Small-fruited banana peppers and hybrid Caribbean types, such as 'Gypsy', are dependable in a wide range of climates.

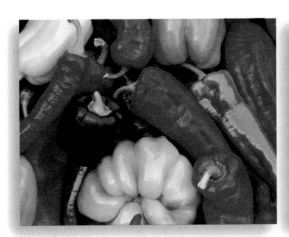

Many hot peppers, such as cayennes and squat "squash" peppers (right) have thin walls, which makes it easy to dry them whole. Fleshier peppers like jalapeños and New Mexican varieties (left) take longer

POTATOES
Solanum tuberosum

POTATO FACTS

Site: Full sun. Well-drained, light, deep, soil high in organic matter. pH 4.8–5.5. Plentiful, consistent moisture. Cool climates best (65°–70° F), but adaptable.

Planting: Cut seed potatoes into pieces, each containing one eye or growing point. Dry the pieces on a tray for up to 2 weeks. Plant in shallow, 4-inch-deep trenches with eyes facing up in fall or winter in southern regions, as soon as the soil can be worked in cool climates, and late April to mid-May in northern gardens.

Spacing: 8–10 inches apart in rows 2 feet apart.

Care: As stems grow, "hill" soil loosely around their bases. Repeat several times through the season. Or, cover with clean, weed-free straw. With this method, you need only pull back the straw at the end of the season to harvest tubers.

Harvest: About 6–8 weeks after planting for new potatoes. Do not disturb plant, dig gently along the sides, then replace soil. Wait until tops die down to harvest mature potatoes. Gently loosen and remove soil, harvesting tubers by hand. Dry, then brush off soil.

Storage: In a cool place. Do not expose tubers to sunlight. Discard any green potatoes; cut out green patches before eating.

Peculiarities: Colorado potato beetle, late blight.

Cut large seed potatoes into pieces up to two weeks before planting. This gives the cut surfaces time to dry.

ABOUT POTATOES

Closely spaced potatoes shade each other, which helps keep soil cool and moist. Before the tubers form, mulch plants to protect shallow tubers from exposure to the sun.

Whether their flesh is buttery yellow or snowy white, freshly harvested potatoes have a unique juicy texture that you find only in home-grown potatoes. Growing potatoes is easy, and each plant should produce at least five spuds. If space is limited, try growing them above the ground in large boxes or bins.

GROWING POTATOES

PLANTING: Potatoes are a cool-season crop best planted in early spring, about three weeks before the last frost. In the South, you can also plant them in fall or winter.

You start potatoes from what are called seed potatoes. These are available at local nurseries, but mail-order companies often provide a wider variety selection. Seed potatoes are identical to the potatoes you eat, but they have been inspected and certified to be free of pests and diseases. If you especially like the potatoes you buy at the store, you can use them as seed potatoes. However, these have sometimes been treated to inhibit sprouting.

Before planting seed potatoes, place them on a warm, sunny windowsill for one to three weeks. Warmth makes them break dormancy and start sprouting, and light causes solanine, a chemical compound with a green pigment, to develop just under the skin. While poisonous to humans, solanine protects the plants from insects.

Cultivate a 30-inch-wide double row of light-textured, well-drained soil for planting. Potatoes are more productive when grown in double rows because neighboring plants shade the soil and help keep it cool, a basic requirement for good potato production. When soil temperatures rise above 75° F, plants stop producing tubers.

Plant seed potatoes whole if they are less than 2 inches in diameter. Cut larger ones into chunks so that each piece has at least two sprouting "eyes." Plant the pieces 2 inches deep and 12 inches apart about three weeks before the last spring frost. To protect young plants from frost, cover them at night with an old blanket.

CARE: Potatoes do not need rich fertilizer. Never add fresh manure to the potato bed because it can contribute to problems with potato scab—a fungal disease that causes rough patches to form on potato skins. High pH also contributes to the development of scab. Keeping pH in the 4.8 to 5.8 range helps prevent the disease.

As soon as their leafy tips appear, begin mulching plants with hay, straw, shredded leaves, or grass clippings. (Take care to use a material free of weed seeds.) Add more mulch as needed to maintain a blanket of organic material at least 3 inches deep. Mulch helps keep the soil cool and moist, discourages pests, and protects shallow tubers from the sun.

Most potato varieties flower in early summer. Pinching off the flowers may help the plants produce a little better, but it is not necessary. Red-skinned varieties have pink blossoms, those with purple skins bloom in lavender, and tan-skinned potatoes form white flowers. Some varieties rarely flower.

HARVEST: When new growth slows and older leaves begin to yellow, gently pull back the mulch and gather tender new potatoes that have formed close to the surface. (Technically, all potatoes gathered from plants with green leaves are new potatoes.) Put the mulch back and leave in place until plants show clear signs of dying back.

To harvest potatoes, loosen soil outside the row with a digging fork, then pull up the plants. Always harvest potatoes on a cloudy day and protect them from exposure to light to prevent solanine production. Some varieties develop small green, tomato-like fruit aboveground. Like potatoes exposed to light, these small fruit contain solanine and should never be eaten.

You can leave potatoes in the ground for a few weeks after the tops have withered, but be sure to pile on extra mulch to protect the tubers from exposure to strong sunlight.

STORAGE: Store harvested potatoes in a cool, dry place. A cellar is ideal, or you can keep them in a cooler sunk into the ground with mulch piled on top to insulate it from the sun. At room temperature, potatoes may break dormancy and begin to sprout after a few weeks. To preserve potatoes that have begun to sprout, blanch and freeze them.

SELECTIONS

Potatoes stop producing new tubers when the soil warms up in summer. For that reason, it is important to choose varieties suited to your climate.

In warm climates where the spring season is short, grow only fast-maturing varieties. Potatoes that mature in 60 to 70 days after planting include 'Red Norland' (red skin, white flesh), 'Caribe' (purple skin, white flesh), and 'Yukon Gold' (tan

skin, yellow flesh). Planting corn or another tall crop to shade potatoes in early summer also may improve yields in warm climates.

In areas with long springs, plant both early and midseason potatoes. The midseason group includes a wide selection of colors and types. Some of the more popular strains are oblong 'Desiree' (red skin, yellow flesh), round 'Red Gold' (red skin, yellow flesh), and several unusual varieties that are purplish-blue throughout the tuber.

Late-maturing potatoes, such as large russet baking potatoes, develop best in northern gardens where 50° to 60° F nights prevail all summer.

Small fingerling potatoes are fun to grow and worth a try in any climate. Most are rated as late maturing, but they produce so many small tubers that you will get a good crop even where the potato season is short. 'Rose Finn Apple' is a disease-resistant fingerling with pink skin that stores well.

Mustard-yellow with black stripes, adult Colorado potato beetles are ½ inch long. They lay clusters of bright orange eggs on the undersides of potato leaves. From these eggs hatch brick-red soft-bodied larvae, sometimes called potato bugs, which have an insatiable appetite for potato leaves and flowers.

Handpick both larvae and adults if there are only a few. Be sure to check plants every few days for new infestations. Where the problem is severe, treat plants with a special strain of *Bacillus thuringiensis* (Bt) developed for this pest or use a neem-based insecticide such as Neem-Away or Bioneem. Floating row covers also protect plants from the beetle.

Growing your own potatoes may be the only way to taste colorful gourmet varieties like these.

Pull salad radishes promptly after they fill out. If left in the ground too long, their texture and flavor decline quickly.

RADISHES
Raphanus sativus

RADISH FACTS

Site: Full sun to part shade. Well-drained, loose soil high in organic matter, free from stones. Plentiful, consistent moisture. Cool weather.
Planting: Direct sow seed 3 weeks before average last frost. Plant every 2 weeks until summer for continuous harvest.
Spacing: ½ inch deep, 1 inch apart in rows 12 inches apart.
Harvest: Pull root when fully formed and tender.
Peculiarities: Cabbage root maggots, flea beetles. Poor quality in hot weather. Heat also intensifies pungency.

ABOUT RADISHES

Crisp, colorful radishes are the fastest growing of all vegetables. They often plump up within a month after sowing. In addition to familiar red radishes, you can enjoy a rainbow of selections with white, purple, or rose-pink skins. Huge oriental Daikon radishes grow so vigorously in the fall that they sometimes are grown as cover crops.

GROWING RADISHES

Daikon radish roots often weigh several pounds. Traditionally, they are preserved by pickling. Daikons seldom have problems with pests, and will grow in any type of soil.

High-quality radishes, which are mild and crisp, require perfect growing conditions: cool weather and constantly moist soil. Harvest them as soon as their roots plump up because hot weather increases their peppery flavor and makes their texture woody.

There are several ways to work radishes into your garden. If you do not consider a salad complete without them, make a series of small, 1-square-foot plantings every two weeks, beginning at the time of your last frost and continuing until days warm to 80° F. Another approach is to mark rows between lettuce, onions, and other spring vegetables with small clumps of radishes. As the larger vegetables gain size, harvest the radishes. A third strategy is to blend the seeds of several varieties together and sow them into a broad bed. Harvesting the earliest variety makes room for the later-maturing plants.

These same strategies work well when growing radishes in fall after nights have become long and the soil has cooled. In most regions, you can sow radishes six weeks or so before your first frost.

Because radishes grow so fast and require constant moisture, plant them in finely cultivated soil that is liberally enriched with organic matter. Sow seeds 1 inch apart and ½ inch deep. In clay soil, cover the seeds with compost or potting soil to promote fast germination. After the seedlings emerge, thin the plants to at least 2 inches apart. Unless radishes are thinned, they will not plump up quickly and evenly.

Keep a watering can handy to lightly moisten the soil every day while radishes are growing and especially when they are nearing maturity. Watch them carefully starting three weeks after planting and pull them as soon as the roots swell to the size of a nickel. In the garden, radishes stay in perfect condition for only a few days. Then they start turning woody.

Problems with flea beetles and cabbage root maggots can be prevented by covering radishes with row covers. Some gardeners use radishes as a companion crop to repel insects that infest squash and cabbage family crops. To test this theory in your garden, grow radishes around these vegetables and allow them to remain in the garden until they flower. Even if you doubt their worth as a pest repellent, you can harvest their tender green seed pods and add them to salads.

SELECTIONS

Salad radishes include numerous round, red types, such as 'Cherry Belle', 'Sparkler', 'Poker', and 'Cherry Bomb'. 'Easter Egg' blend is an assortment of small red, white, and purple radishes. French radishes, such as 'French Breakfast' and 'D'Avignon', grow into 4-inch-long cylinders with white tips and red shoulders. Cylindrical radish varieties also come in all-white or all-red types.

Oriental Daikon radishes produce huge carrot-shaped roots that can weigh several pounds. They are easy to grow in fall but often bolt when grown in spring.

RHUBARB
Rheum × cultorum

A hardy perennial, rhubarb thrives with little care in climates with long, cold winters. It grows in full sun to partial shade.

ABOUT RHUBARB

Rhubarb is a large perennial plant that grows best where winters are cold enough to freeze the ground. In milder areas, grow it only as a winter annual.

The edible part of the rhubarb plant is its thick stalk, below the leaf, which is quite tart until sweetened and cooked. Rhubarb leaves contain toxic levels of oxalic acid and never should be consumed.

GROWING RHUBARB

Rhubarb requires a site in full sun to partial shade with deep, loose, moist soil that is rich in organic matter.

The fastest way to establish plants is to set out purchased dormant roots in spring. Rhubarb grows quite large, so space individual planting holes 3 feet apart.

Dig holes 15 inches deep and 24 inches wide, and mix 2 gallons of compost or rotted manure into each. In porous sandy soil that does not hold nutrients well, add a standard application of a balanced organic or slow-release fertilizer to the bottom of the planting hole.

Set the roots so that the central bud is a scant 1 inch below the soil surface. Cover with soil and water well. In early summer, mulch plants with an organic material to keep the soil cool and moist. Where summers are hot, add mulch as needed to keep it at least 2 inches deep.

Do not harvest rhubarb the first year after planting. Allow it to grow freely. The second year, harvest plants lightly during the first half of summer by twisting off up to six stems per plant. In subsequent years, you can harvest up to 20 stalks per plant, taking a few at a time all summer long. Cut off any flower stalks that develop to help the plant channel its energy to forming stems.

Fertilize rhubarb every spring. Spread rotted manure between plants to a depth of 2 inches, or rake back mulch and spread 1 cup of 10-10-10 fertilizer in a wide circle around each plant. Replace the mulch.

Rhubarb plants may become crowded. If after five or six years their stems are thin rather than thick and juicy, dig and divide the plants in spring or fall. Cut the tough roots into pieces at least 2 inches across, taking care not to injure the buds on the tops of the pieces. Discard roots that are corky or show signs of rotting and immediately replant the best chunks.

An occasional pest to watch for is the rhubarb curculio. To control it, keep the planting area clean—remove weeds and infested crowns and stalks. This removes the pest's overwintering sites.

In areas with mild winters, grow rhubarb as a winter annual or short-lived perennial. Start seeds indoors in late summer. Set out plants when the weather cools in fall. Begin harvesting stalks in late winter.

In marginal areas that have cold winters and hot, humid summers, grow rhubarb in a northern exposure where the plants receive partial shade.

SELECTIONS

The best strains of rhubarb are propagated by division rather than from seed. Green varieties often are the most productive, but many people prefer varieties with colorful red stems. 'Valentine' and 'Crimson Red' are two good choices. 'Victoria' is the most vigorous red-stemmed variety that can be grown from seed.

RHUBARB FACTS

Site: Full sun to part shade. Deep well-drained, fertile soil high in organic matter. Plentiful, consistent moisture. Because this is a long-lived perennial crop, give thought to its location.

Planting: By dormant crowns, as soon as the soil can be worked in spring.

Spacing: 2 inches deep, 3 feet apart.

Care: Mulch. Remove flower stalks as they appear the first year to give strength to developing plant.

Harvest: Do not harvest the year after planting. Harvest only several stalks from individual plants the second year after planting.

Storage: Refrigerate stalks for up to 2 weeks before eating. Do not consume leaves.

Peculiarities: Rhubarb curculios.

Harvest rhubarb by snapping off a few leaf stalks at a time. New stalks grow from the plants' centers. Remove the toxic leaves before chopping the stalks.

ROOT CROPS

Root crops are the convenience food of the garden because they can be left in the ground for several weeks or even months until needed. Where the ground freezes hard in winter, dig most of the roots in late fall and store them in a cool cellar or unheated basement.

JERUSALEM ARTICHOKE

Also known as sunchokes, Jerusalem artichoke (*Helianthus tuberosus*) is a perennial sunflower with sweet, nutty roots. They look like knobby potatoes and can be eaten raw or cooked.

This native-American vegetable thrives in any type of soil. Plant it in spring in a corner of the garden where the 6- to 8-foot-tall plants will not shade other crops.

Small yellow sunflowers appear in late summer. You can harvest roots anytime after the soil cools, but a few hard freezes improve their nutty flavor.

Store a few starter roots for the next season in a 12-inch-deep hole dug in the ground and harvest the rest as needed all winter. In midspring, check the area where you grew this crop the year before and dig out unwanted plants. If allowed to naturalize, Jerusalem artichokes may become invasive.

Towering Jerusalem artichokes' flowers appear in late summer. Harvest plants in late fall.

hairy in nitrogen-rich soil, so add no fertilizer before planting.

Plant the seeds in late spring to early summer or in fall about 90 days before the first frost. Germination usually takes two to three weeks. Buy fresh seed every year to improve chances of good germination.

Plant seeds 1 inch apart in ½-inch-deep furrows and fill the furrows with compost to keep a crust from forming over the seeds. Cover the rows with boards for 7 to 10 days to maintain constant soil moisture. After removing the cover, water frequently to keep the soil moist until the sprouts appear. Thin the seedlings to 4 to 6 inches apart when they are about 1 month old.

Begin harvesting parsnips in mid- to late fall, after the soil has cooled and several frosts

JERUSALEM ARTICHOKE FACTS

Site: Full sun, well-drained soil. Takes a range of sites and soils.
Planting: Cut large tubers into pieces or plant individual tubers in spring, 2 weeks before last frost.
Spacing: 3 inches deep, 18 inches apart.
Care: Remove yellow flowers the first year to give strength to plant. Keep moist in dry periods.
Harvest: Dig tubers after leaves die back in the fall, leaving some for the next season.
Peculiarities: No major insect pests or diseases. Can become invasive unless you make sure to harvest all tubers.

PARSNIP FACTS

Site: Full sun to part shade. Moist, well-drained, loose, fertile soil.
Planting: Direct seed 2–3 weeks before average last frost.
Spacing: ½ inch deep, ½ inch apart, rows 18 inches apart. Thin to 4 inches.
Care: Cut thinnings so as not to disturb nearby roots. Mulch.
Harvest: After frost. Dig roots all at once or mulch plants and pull as needed through winter. Days to harvest: 90–120.
Storage: For 2 weeks in plastic bag in refrigerator or for several months in cool, moist root cellar.
Peculiarities: Root maggots.

PARSNIP

Parsnips (*Pastinaca sativa*) are not related to carrots, but the two crops have much in common: They share a similar shape and crisp texture. But white parsnip roots have a distinctive nutty flavor that sweetens and mellows after cooking.

Grow parsnips in deeply worked, fertile, loamy soil in full sun or partial shade or in raised beds if your soil is clay.

Like carrots, parsnips will become forked and

Begin harvesting parsnips in fall after the soil has cooled. Leave some in the ground to dig as you need them through winter.

have occurred. Chilly soil brings out the sweetness in parsnip roots and also improves their texture. You can leave mature roots in the ground all winter and dig them as you need them until early spring. To make digging easier, mulch plants with a foot of straw or shredded leaves in early winter. Parsnips are biennial and die early in their second year.

TURNIP

A staple fall crop in the South, turnips (*Brassica rapa*) are versatile vegetables. Steam the leaves as greens, chop fresh roots into salads, or store mature roots for winter meals.

All varieties offer flavorful leaves to use as cooking greens. For salads, fast-maturing Oriental varieties develop almost as quickly as radishes. Large, slow-growing varieties which have a smooth texture and full-bodied flavor after cooking are best for winter storage.

Plant turnips in full sun to partial shade. Soil should be rich, fertile, and high in organic matter. You can grow salad turnips and greens in both spring and fall, but turnips for storage are best grown in autumn. Flavor becomes bitter in warm temperatures.

Turnip seeds germinate fast. Plant them ½ inch deep and 2 inches apart. When plants are 3 inches tall, thin them to 5 inches apart. Thinnings make flavorful cooking greens.

Harvest turnip greens by pulling individual leaves, or use a knife to cut handfuls of leaves 1 inch above the plant crowns. Water the plants after harvesting them, and they will quickly produce a flush of new leaves. Harvest only a few greens from the plants you are growing for storage.

Dig roots as you need them when they are at least 3 inches across. Harvest all remaining roots before temperatures drop below 25° F,

because hard freezes can split them and make them woody.

Sweet salad turnips need constant moisture while growing and are best harvested when they are less than 2 inches in diameter.

Try 'Hakurei' for sweet salad turnips, 'Shogoin' for tender turnips and greens, and 'Purple Top White Globe' for storage. 'Gilfeather' forms a large, sweet root with green top.

RUTABAGA

Rutabagas (*Brassica napus*) grow much like turnips, although the plants are quite different. Rutabaga leaves are inedible; their roots are larger than turnips'. Texture is dense and flavor slightly sweet.

For the best flavor and texture, keep soil evenly moist. Plants are cold hardy and can be left in the ground through winter in many areas.

In cold areas, plant rutabagas 90 days before cold weather sets in. Sow seeds 2 inches apart in fertile, well-drained soil with a near-neutral pH. In mild-winter areas, plant seeds in early fall after nights have cooled to 50° to 60° F. Thin seedlings to 8 inches apart when they are 4 inches tall.

Aphids can be a problem. Hose off plants to remove them or spray with insecticidal soap.

Wait to harvest rutabaga roots until after several frosts. Chilling improves their flavor. In early winter, trim the tops of remaining plants and mulch them to make them easier to harvest during winter.

Varieties differ mostly in terms of color and disease resistance. 'Marian', which resists clubroot disease, and 'Joan' develop yellow-fleshed roots with purple tops. 'York Swede' is another clubroot-resistant variety.

Rutabagas have a dense texture and rich flavor that sets them apart from other root vegetables.

TURNIP FACTS

Site: Full sun to part shade. Deep, well-drained, loose soil of average fertility without stones, high in organic matter. Plentiful moisture. Cool.
Planting: Direct sow 4–6 weeks before last frost. Sow in late summer for fall harvest; in fall for winter harvest in South.
Spacing: ½ inch deep, ½ inch apart, in rows 12 inches apart. Thin to 5 inches.
Care: Mulch. Avoid excess nitrogen.
Harvest: Pull when roots 1–2 inches in diameter. Leaves are also edible. Days to harvest: 35–75.
Peculiarities: Flea beetles, aphids, root maggots.

RUTABAGA FACTS

Site: See turnip.
Planting: Direct seed 4–6 weeks before average last frost. For fall crop, sow seed in late summer in northern regions, in fall in southern regions. Mulch.
Spacing: ½ inch deep, 2 inches apart in rows 18–24 inches apart. Thin to 8 inches.
Harvest: Dig roots as needed when about 4 inches in diameter. Days to harvest: about 90.
Peculiarities: Clubroot disease, aphids, flea beetles.

Turnip roots grow at the soil surface. Gather young leaves for cooking greens, use roots fresh in salads, or store them for winter stews.

SALAD GREENS

If you enjoy salads and like to sample unusual flavors, set aside a few square feet of your spring and fall garden for European salad greens. All are cool-season crops, and some are winter hardy.

Flavor varies with species. Endives and chicories have a distinct bitter edge, while mâche is mild and nutty.

Keep plantings small as you experiment to find personal favorites. You can also make your own blend of strong-flavored greens and traditional leafy vegetables, such as lettuce and spinach. In addition to the greens discussed on these pages, arugula, beet greens, and tender young mustard help round out any salad.

Salad greens require a sunny, well-drained site and moderately fertile soil. Endive can tolerate partial shade. Before planting—especially greens that will remain in the garden all winter—mix a balanced organic or slow-release fertilizer into the soil. After planting, water regularly for steady plant growth. Keeping soil constantly moist and harvesting leaves when they are young and tender are the secrets to growing fine salad greens.

This spirited mesclun mixture includes endive, mustard, and red- and green-leafed lettuces. Mesclun is always best when harvested as baby greens, so make several small sowings in spring and again in the fall. Provide plenty of water to promote fast, steady growth.

keep it moist while they germinate.

When leaves are 3 inches long (usually about a month after sowing), harvest mesclun by cutting handfuls of green leaves 1 inch above the soil surface. Scissors or a sharp knife work well.

Water after harvesting to help plants quickly produce a fresh crop. Each sowing will provide at least three cuttings. To assure a constant supply, sow at least three bands of mesclun each spring, two weeks apart, and several more at two-week intervals in fall.

LOOKING FOR RUTABAGAS?
See page 77.

MESCLUN

Mesclun is a concept rather than a vegetable. It is a blend of young salad greens, which can be mild, spicy, or bitter depending on the plants you include in the mixture. It is a good way to get to know salad greens without buying many different packets of seed.

Mild mesclun blends usually consist mostly of leaf lettuce, with small amounts of more flavorful greens such as endive, arugula, and chervil. Spicy mixtures often include mustards instead of lettuce. Usually, they are so spicy that they are best mixed with lettuce in a salad.

To grow mesclun, make a ½-inch-deep trench 2 inches wide and 12 inches long and lightly scatter the seeds so that they are spaced about ½ inch apart. Cover them with ¼ inch of soil and

MESCLUN FACTS
Site: Full sun to part shade. Well-drained, rich soil, high in organic matter. Cool, moist weather.
Planting: Direct sow in rows, bands or broadcast in patches as soon as soil can be worked in spring. Continue planting every two weeks for continuous harvest. For fall crops, sow in midsummer in northern regions, late summer to fall in southern areas. Grow in cold frames for winter harvest.
Spacing: ¼ inch deep in rows 18 to 24 inches apart. Thin to 10 inches. Can also sow.
Care: Mulch. Suspend shade cloth over plants with stakes or hoops to help crops through heat of summer.
Harvest: As needed when leaves are 4–6 inches long. Remove outer leaves of plants or cut at the base with a sharp knife.
Peculiarities: Will bolt—go to seed—in heat.

MÂCHE

Also known as lamb's lettuce or corn salad, mâche (*Valerianella locusta*) is a mild-flavored green that is extremely tolerant of cold weather. Unlike most other salad greens, dark green mâche leaves have a tame flavor and buttery texture similar to butterhead lettuce. The plants often get lost in mesclun mixtures because of their tendency to hug the ground. It will be easier to keep track of if you plant mâche on its own in early fall.

Sow the seeds in a pattern to make it easy to distinguish the seedlings from weeds. Plant seeds ½ inch deep and ½ inch apart. Thin them to 2 inches. Most varieties produce glossy, spoon-shaped leaves that emerge from the plants' centers in a circular pattern. Some produce tufts of leaves on short stems.

Mâche

Harvest mâche by pinching off leaf clusters after the plants have grown into circular rosettes that are at least 3 inches across. Cold weather enhances the sweet, nutty flavor of mâche, and plants often retain their quality well into spring. In areas where winters are severe, cover mâche with a sturdy plastic tunnel in late fall.

ENDIVE

Endive (*Cichorium endivia*) closely resembles leaf lettuce in appearance and vigor, and it is planted at the same times in spring and fall. Like lettuce, hot weather turns endive bitter. Unlike lettuce, endive's flavor is sharp and almost peppery. It tolerates cold weather better than lettuce. Endive grows in full sun to partial shade.

In the North, direct seed endive 4 weeks before the last frost. Plant seed ¼ inch deep and 2 inches apart, and thin to 12 inches when leaves are a few inches high. In the South, sow seed in the late summer.

You can harvest young endive as baby salad greens or allow plants to mature. When mature, endive forms large, loose heads with white to light lime green central hearts. Leaf veins are stiff and crisp, and edges usually are finely cut and curled, but they can be feathery or flat.

Young endive plants.

Sometimes called frisée, mature endive is often blanched for two weeks prior to harvest. This helps retain the creamy white color in the plants' crisp centers. To blanch, tie the outer leaves into a bundle over the hearts and hold it in place with string, a rubber band, or twist ties.

Escarole is the same species as endive, but it has wide, scalloped leaves and slightly milder flavor than endive. It is sometimes called broadleaf endive. Escarole is best when it matures in cool fall weather. Mature escarole hearts are often served lightly braised. Cooking reduces their bitterness and helps bring out their sweet flavor.

CHICORY

There are two types of chicory (*Cichorium intybus*): cutting chicory and perennial chicory, which is also called radicchio. Both are bitter plants that lend a bite to salads.

Cutting chicory is cultivated much like leaf lettuce. Harvest leaves when they are 4 to 5 inches long by snipping them off 1 inch above plant crowns. To harvest older plants that have developed small heads, pull up the entire plant, discard older leaves, and keep only the tender center rosette.

Cutting chicory

Perennial chicory is grown primarily for its pale, crisp heart. Most varieties are bright red and are valued as much for their color as for their bitter flavor. Like many bitter greens, the flavor of perennial chicory is an acquired taste.

Plants grow into a large mounded mass of broad leaves. Tender cone-shaped hearts develop when plants are nearly mature, which may be in late fall or early spring. Sow seeds in late summer, spacing then 1 inch apart. Thin the seedlings to 8 inches apart. Mulch between plants to control weeds and to keep soil evenly moist. Harvest when plants develop firm central heads.

Perennial chicory

In many areas, radicchio will survive winter and produce again in spring. You can coax overwintered plants that have become ragged into producing pretty heads by cutting off the tops 2 inches above the crown in early spring. Small heads should appear within a month.

Several bolt-resistant varieties are available, including 'Giulio' (dense, red heads), 'Rossana' (dark red), and 'Scilla' (round red). You don't need to cut these varieties back for them to form heads.

CHICORY FACTS

Site: Full sun to part shade. Well-drained, rich soil high in organic matter. Plentiful moisture.
Planting: Direct sow 4 to 6 weeks before last frost.
Spacing: ½ inch deep, 1 inch apart in rows 24 inches apart. Thin to 10 inches.
Care: Mulch. Let plants grow through summer, then cut them back in fall. Red heads will form, which you can harvest in a month. Days to harvest: 55–100.
Harvest: When heads are full and slightly firm. Leave the crown; it may form a second flush of growth the next spring.
Peculiarities: Can be unpredictable. May send a flush of edible leaves instead of forming heads.

ENDIVE FACTS

Site: Full sun to part shade. Well-drained, fertile, loose soil high in organic matter. Plentiful, consistent moisture. More heat tolerant than many salad greens.
Planting: Direct sow 4 weeks before last frost. For fall crop, sow in midsummer in north and late summer to fall in south.
Spacing: ¼ inch deep in rows 18 inches apart. Thin to 10 inches.
Care: Mulch. For milder flavor, blanch leaves by pulling them together and holding with twist ties. Self-blanching varieties are available.
Harvest: Cut young plants off at base. Older plants become bitter.
Peculiarities: Aphids. Bitter in hot weather.

SPINACH
Spinacia oleracea

'Space' is a smooth-leafed spinach that grows upright, which helps to keep leaves clean.

ABOUT SPINACH

Crisp spinach leaves turn everyday salads into special treats. Or cook fresh spinach and enjoy its rich, buttery texture.

SPINACH FACTS

Site: Full sun to part shade. Well-drained, fertile soil high in organic matter. Plentiful, consistent moisture. Tolerates slightly alkaline soil.

Planting: Sow seed in spring as soon as soil can be worked. Make succession plantings every 2 weeks until warm weather arrives. Sow again in late summer in northern regions, fall in southern regions.

Spacing: ½ inch deep, 1 inch apart in rows 18 inches apart, or broadcast seed. Thin to 6 inches.

Care: Mulch soil to maintain moisture. Lightly sidedress with nitrogen-based fertilizer to speed growth.

Harvest: Pick individual leaves as needed.

Peculiarities: Mildew, slugs, leaf miners. Cool-season crop prone to bolting in heat. Leaves become bitter after bolting.

Spinach tolerates temperatures as low as 10° F. Heavily curled savoyed varieties stand up to the rigors of winter especially well.

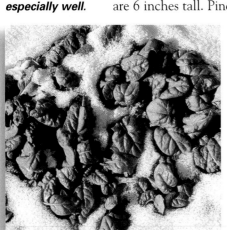

GROWING SPINACH

Spinach craves cool weather and can withstand cold temperatures to at least 10° F. Plant it in early spring and again in fall. Fall-planted spinach planted often survives through winter and produces a second crop the following spring.

Grow spinach in full sun or partial shade in rich soil with a near-neutral pH. However, spinach can adapt to slightly acidic conditions provided you supply it with plenty of nitrogen. Spinach requires more nitrogen than most other crops. Mix a high-nitrogen fertilizer or a 2-inch-deep layer of composted manure into the soil before planting.

Soak seeds overnight. Then plant them in the garden the next day, sowing them ½ inch deep and 1 inch apart. Thin seedlings to 6 inches apart when plants have three or four leaves. Mulch spinach plants to help keep their leaves clean and soil moist.

With spring-sown spinach, begin harvesting individual leaves when the plants are 6 inches tall. Pinch off two to three leaves per plant. Harvested this way, you can pick spinach from individual plants about once every 10 days.

The habit of spinach is more compact when grown in the fall. Also, leaves tend to be thicker and crisper.

Harvest fall-sown spinach just as you would in spring, but stop picking it when growth slows in early winter. Instead, protect the plants from ice with a light mulch or grow them through the winter under plastic tunnels. As soon as the soil warms in spring, overwintered spinach will again begin to grow and produce a heavy crop of sweet, crunchy leaves.

When new growth begins in spring, sidedress the plants with composted manure or douse them with fish emulsion or another high-nitrogen liquid fertilizer.

Spinach stops growing leaves when days lengthen in spring. Instead, the plants grow tall and flower. Pull up plants when this happens because their leaves will quickly lose their good flavor and texture.

Leaf miners can be a problem on spinach. To control this pest, remove affected leaves and destroy them. Don't toss the leaves onto the compost pile. The insects can escape and return to your garden.

SELECTIONS

Smooth-leaf spinach varieties, such as 'Space', produce tender, thin leaves on upright stems. However, they do not hold up well to ice and snow. They are best grown in spring. Many smooth-leafed varieties are slow to bolt. 'Olympia' is both mildew and bolt resistant.

Semi-savoyed varieties have leaves that are slightly crinkled. They also have thicker leaves and produce well in spring or fall. 'Tyee' is a downey mildew-resistant semi-savoyed variety. 'Melody' resists mosaic as well as powdery mildew.

Savoyed spinach, such as 'Bloomsdale Longstanding', has thick, heavily crinkled leaves. It holds up well to winter weather and makes an outstanding fall and winter crop.

SQUASH AND PUMPKIN
Cucurbita pepo, C. maxima, C. moschata

Summer squash has a thin rind. This group includes zucchini, yellow straightneck, and patty pan squash.

SQUASH AND PUMPKIN FACTS

Site: Full sun. Well-drained, fertile, loose soil high in organic matter. Plentiful consistent moisture from the time plants emerge until fruit begins to fill out. Warm.

Planting: Seed directly or transplant seedlings. Sow seed indoors, 1 inch deep in peat pots 3 weeks before setting out. Set out 2 weeks after average last frost date. (Old-fashioned "Three Sisters" method of planting vining squashes and pumpkins: Plant squash in every seventh hill of dent, flour, or flint corn. Allow the third "sister," pole beans, to climb the corn.)

Spacing: Four to five squash seeds per hill. Six to seven pumpkin seeds per hill. Hills 4 feet apart. Thin to three plants per hill. You can also plant squash in rows. Bush squashes: 20 inches apart in rows 24 inches apart. Vining squashes: 20 inches apart in rows 4 feet apart. Pumpkins: 3 feet apart in rows 8 feet apart.

Care: Black-plastic or organic mulch. Trellis in small gardens.

Harvest: Harvest summer squash while young and tender. Zucchini, crookneck, and straightneck squashes: when young, tender, and no more than 6–8 inches long. Pattypan squash: while small and pale. Winter squash and pumpkins: before first fall frost. Cut off fruit, leaving some stem. Tissues of winter squash and pumpkins will break down if exposed to frost. Cure in warm, dry place for several days before storing in a cool, dry spot. Days to harvest: 45–120.

Peculiarities: Bacterial wilt, cucumber beetles, squash vine borers, mosaic virus, mildew. Sensitive to frost.

ABOUT SQUASH

Squash and pumpkins are closely related members of the cucumber family. Native to the warm regions of North America, these vigorous plants grow quickly and are among the most productive and nutritious vegetables you can grow.

Two groups of vegetables go by the name of squash: One has soft, easily punctured skin. These are the summer squashes, which include zucchini, Lebanese, pattypan, crookneck, and straightneck squash. The other group is composed of winter squashes. These have hard, thick rinds, which makes them suitable for long-term storage. Among the winter squashes are acorn, butternut, banana, and hubbard squash.

Pumpkins and most types of winter squash require plenty of room for their long, wandering vines. Summer squash have a more compact, bushy habit, which makes them a better fit for small gardens.

SUMMER SQUASH

Green zucchini squash are phenomenally productive and include numerous hybrids with blackish green, gray-green, striped, or yellow rinds, all of which are an interesting addition to the garden. Bulbous, light green Lebanese squash are similar to zucchinis and have a natural tolerance for insects and diseases. Yellow squash can have either curved or straight necks, depending on variety. Straightneck hybrids are reliably productive, but many gardeners prefer crooknecks for their appearance and flavor.

Scallop or pattypan squash are shaped like flattened flowers and add variety to summer gardens. Their colors range from yellow, greenish white to white.

PEST WATCH
SQUASH BUGS

Beginning in early summer, squash bugs suck the sap from leaves and stems of squash and pumpkin plants. The ⅔-inch-long adults are a mottled brown color with flat backs and orange markings under their wings. They lay glossy brown eggs on leaves in precise groups. Ten days later, small gray nymphs hatch and begin to feed.

Handpick squash bugs as soon as they appear. Thoroughly wetting the plants often makes the adults move to the tops of the plants, where they are easy to gather. Pyrethrum or another garden pesticide labeled for use on squash will help bring severe infestations under control. A row cover over plants also protects squash from these bugs.

SQUASH AND PUMPKIN
continued

GROWING SUMMER SQUASH

For a head start on the season, you can plant summer squash indoors in containers at about the time of your last frost. Transplant the seedlings three weeks later when soil warms. Or direct sow seed 1 inch deep 6 inches apart in fertile soil starting two weeks after your last frost. Thin the seedlings to 2 feet apart after they develop at least 2 large leaves.

The first flowers that appear (usually 40 to 50 days after planting) are infertile males. Female flowers, which develop a week or so later, set fruit when fertilized by pollen from male flowers. In small plantings, hand-pollinating by brushing pollen from male flowers into the centers of female blooms often improves fruit set. To keep the harvest interesting, grow several types of summer squash but only a few plants of each. If you intend to save seeds, be aware that because summer squash are all the same species, they can cross-pollinate one another.

Harvest summer squash when the fruit is young and tender, cutting it off with a sharp knife. Leave a bit of green stem attached to the plant. Squash blossoms are edible, too, and make colorful additions to many dishes. Baby squash harvested with their blossoms attached are a delicacy. Promptly remove overripe fruit from the plants to encourage the development of new flowers and fruit.

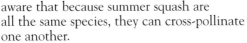

Insects carrying pollen grains fertilize female squash and pumpkin flowers, then fruit begins to grow. In small plantings, you can improve fruit set by pollinating plants yourself using a small paintbrush to distribute pollen to female flowers. You can tell male flowers by their smooth, thin stems. Female flowers have a green bulge that looks like a miniature fruit at the base of their petals.

WINTER SQUASH

Winter squash will store for several weeks—or even months—if you harvest it when its skin is hard and the seeds inside are fully mature.

Acorn squash requires a little less space than other types of winter squash. Butternuts are highly tolerant of pests, and their flavor often becomes sweeter after they have been in storage for several weeks. Buttercup squash, known as sweet potato squash because of its rich flavor, makes terrific pies. Delicata squash is ideal for stuffing and baking.

Huge hubbards store for a long time. Other winter squashes include spaghetti, golden nugget, kabocha, and turban squash.

Winter squash have thick rinds suitable for long-term storage. They include acorn, butternut, hubbard, and turban squashes.

GROWING WINTER SQUASH

Choose a site with full sun and well-drained, fertile, deep soil that is high in organic matter. Winter squash needs consistent and plentiful moisture.

To grow a low-maintenance planting of winter squash, plan ahead. Work 1 cup of 10-10-10 fertilizer into each planting hill or apply 25 pounds of 10-10-10 per 1,000 square feet of row space. Cover the area with black plastic mulch. The plastic will raise the soil temperature, conserve moisture, reduce weeds, and keep the fertilizer from washing away.

Cut holes in the plastic 3 to 4 feet apart for planting seeds. Sow three to five seeds in each hole. Two weeks later, thin the seedlings to two per hole. You can also set out transplants one to two weeks after the last frost date.

Where summers are cool or insect problems are severe, cover plants with a row cover until female blossoms appear. Remove the cover to let insects in to pollinate flowers. In small plantings, you can assist pollination by spreading the pollen by hand. After each plant has at least four green fruit, replace the row cover, but first handpick insects or treat plants with a general garden pesticide.

Winter squash are ready to harvest when the fruit has a firm rind that is difficult to pierce with your fingernail. By then the plants usually appear ragged as well. Harvest fruit by cutting it from the vine with a sharp knife or pruning shears and leaving a short stub of stem attached. Wipe it clean with a damp cloth and store in a cool, dry place.

SELECTIONS

Try different varieties to keep your harvest of summer squash more colorful and interesting. Hybrid summer squash are more prolific than open-pollinated varieties, so more squash grows in less space. Most popular varieties, such as 'Dixie' yellow crookneck, 'Embassy' green zucchini, and bright yellow 'Sunburst' pattypan are hybrids.

Where insect or disease problems are severe, try vigorous Lebanese squash varieties, such as 'Kuta', 'Zahra', or 'Clarimore'. These can outproduce zucchinis.

For winter squash, buttercup varieties like 'Sweet Mama' produce heavy crops, but they are susceptible to squash vine borers. The

Pumpkins range from tiny miniatures you use for decorating to prize-winning giants that require a forklift to move. Besides orange, pumpkins can have gray, green-and-yellow striped, white, tan, and buff rinds. Also, pumpkin skin may be smooth, ribbed, furrowed, or warty.

larvae of this moth burrows into stems. Plants wilt suddenly and eventually die. Sawdust-like frass is a telltale sign of the borers. Butternuts, which are a different species (*C. moschata*), are seldom bothered by this pest.

Spaghetti squash, whose cooked flesh resembles pasta, is a favorite. Petite delicata or dumpling squash have the sweet potato flavor of butternuts and are the perfect size for cutting in half and baking or stuffing.

ABOUT PUMPKINS

Pumpkins are a type of winter squash. They range in size from 3-inch miniatures to giant thunderbellies weighing several hundred pounds. The best for eating are 5- to 10-pound pie pumpkins, which you can use as decorations before cooking.

Pumpkins with bright orange rinds are popular for carving, but the less common gray or white pumpkins offer variety.

GROWING PUMPKINS

Plant pumpkins in late spring in cool-summer climates. In warmer areas, plant them in early to midsummer so fruit will mature in fall. Pumpkins develop long vines, which benefit from filtered shade in midsummer. Growing them near sweet corn or along a fence provides the shade. As the vines ramble through the corn patch or along fence rows, their huge leaves shade out weeds.

To protect ripening fruit from insects and soil-borne diseases, place a piece of cardboard or folded newspaper between the fruit and bare soil.

To grow giant pumpkins, you'll need at least three plants of a large-fruited variety of *C. maxima*, such as 'Big Moon' or 'Atlantic Giant', which technically, is not a pumpkin but a squash. After the fruit sets, clip off all but one or two of the largest, shapeliest fruit. With regular watering, you should harvest pumpkins weighing at least 50 pounds each.

Leave pumpkins on the plants until the vines begin to turn yellow and die back. Mature pumpkins may be kept outside through light fall frosts, but bring them in before hard freezes commence. Store pumpkins in a cool, dry place after wiping them clean with a damp cloth.

SELECTIONS

'Jack Be Little' is a decorative miniature pumpkin, no more than 3 inches in diameter. Good pumpkins for pies are 'Lumina', which is a white pumpkin, and 'Small Sugar'. If you want to grow pumpkins for the edible seeds, choose a hull-less or semi-hull-less variety, such as 'Baby Bear'.

For huge, prize-winning pumpkins plant large-fruited varieties such as 'Atlantic Giant'.

SWEET POTATO
Ipomoea batatas

SWEET POTATO FACTS

Site: Full sun. Well-drained, deep, light-textured soil, free of stones. Plentiful, consistent moisture.

Planting: By rooted "slips," or by cut sections of tuber each with at least one growing point. Start tubers indoors 6 weeks before last frost. Plant them 2 inches deep in moist vermiculite. Keep in a warm, sunny location. After sprouting, add another inch of vermiculite. Transplant 2–3 weeks after average last frost in flattened hills of soil, three slips per hill. Plant them with the rooted side pointing down.

Spacing: 3 feet.

Care: Mulch. Do not use high-nitrogen fertilizers.

Harvest: Gently dig tubers after first frost. Do not bruise or break tender skins. Cure in warm sun for several hours, then place tubers loosely in paper bags and allow to further cure for 1 week in a warm, dry area. Days to harvest: 90–120.

Storage: In cool, dry location.

Peculiarities: Fusarium wilt, wireworms, weevils. Not as troubled in northern regions.

'Vardaman' sweet potatoes have smooth, heart-shaped leaves on short vines.

ABOUT SWEET POTATOES

Packed with nutrition, sweet potatoes grow in areas where warm weather lasts at least three months. The vining plants form a lovely green ground cover, and each one produces four or more sweet tubers.

GROWING SWEET POTATOES

Actually tropical perennials, sweet potatoes will grow in northern gardens if you pre-warm the soil with black plastic mulch before planting. Raised beds also warm up earlier in spring and are suitable for sweet potatoes.

Plant sweet potatoes in a sunny site with well-drained soil and a pH between 5.5 and 6.5. Before planting, enrich the site with a 1-inch-deep layer of compost or low-nitrogen fertilizer.

Start your sweet potato patch with 6-inch-long rooted stems called slips. Buy certified disease-free slips in late spring or grow your own by placing sweet potatoes vertically in jars of water on a warm windowsill. Each potato will produce two to four leafy stems with a few stringy roots. These roots are the slips. Break off and plant the slips when they reach 4 to 6 inches long.

After the soil warms to 70° F, plant slips diagonally in 4-inch-deep furrows so that only the top three leaves show at the soil surface. Allow 16 inches between plants and 36 inches between

Harvest sweet potatoes when they grow to the size you like. Be aware, though, that oversize tubers often have stringy fibers.

rows. Water slips after planting and keep them constantly moist for at least a week. Plants will need an inch of water per week to keep tubers from cracking.

Begin checking your crop 80 days after planting, and harvest roots when they swell to 3 inches across. If left in the ground too long, some varieties grow gigantic roots with a stringy, fibrous texture. All sweet potatoes stop growing when the soil temperature drops to near 55° F in fall.

To harvest sweet potatoes, loosen the soil outside the row with a digging fork, then pull on the crown of the vines. Brush off soil from the tubers (avoid damaging their delicate skin). Cure the tubers at 80° F for 10 days. As their skins cure, sweet potatoes will toughen, and small scratches and harvesting wounds "heal" over. After curing, gently clean the tubers again and allow them to continue drying for a few days. Store cured sweet potatoes in a dry, cool place where the temperature remains around 60° F.

SELECTIONS

Where summers are short, grow fast-maturing 'Georgia Jet'. In warm climates, long-vined 'Centennial' and 'Beauregarde' produce high yields of excellent sweet potatoes with deep orange flesh. 'Porto Rico' and 'Vardaman' with their short vines are great choices for small gardens.

Unusual white-fleshed sweet potatoes, such as 'White Triumph' and 'Sumor', make interesting crops and are as easy to grow as orange-fleshed varieties.

TOMATO
Lycopersicon esculentum

Support tomatoes in a sturdy enclosure before they are heavy with fruit. This is 'Champion', a tasty, disease-resistant hybrid.

TOMATO FACTS

Site: Full sun. Well-drained, fertile soil high in organic matter. Tolerates slightly acid soil. Consistent moisture prevents blossom-end rot.

Planting: Sow seeds indoors, 6–8 weeks before transplanting. Plant outside 1–2 weeks after average last frost.

Spacing: ⅛ inch deep, 2–3 feet apart.

Care: Stake or trellis indeterminate varieties. Staking is optional for determinates. Pinch off side shoots that appear where branches and stems meet. Mulch to maintain soil moisture. Supply consistent moisture when rainfall is less than 1 inch per week.

Harvest: As fruit ripens and is firm and fully-colored. Before the first frost, harvest all full-sized green fruit that are nearly mature. Set in a warm location to continue ripening. Days to harvest: 50-80.

Peculiarities: Tomato hornworms, blossom end rot, early blight, and late blight.

ABOUT TOMATOES

Gardeners are passionate about tomatoes, the most popular vegetable in the summer garden. Successfully growing them is simple: Choose varieties suited to your climate and do everything you can to help the plants to grow steadily and without interruption.

Many of the ways you handle tomatoes when growing them is determined by their growth habit, which may be determinate, vigorous determinate, or indeterminate. You'll find this information on the seed packet or plant identification tags, and in seed catalog descriptions.

DETERMINATE TOMATOES: Determinate varieties grow into bushy plants that need no support and develop clusters of blossoms and fruit at the stem tips. They mature early and ripen within one to two weeks, so they are ideal for canning or freezing and for growing in short-season areas. Generally, the fruit ripens over a concentrated period of time, usually three weeks, then the plants die.

VIGOROUS DETERMINATES: Vigorous determinates, also called semi-determinates, produce a heavy crop all at once, but they do not die afterward. If you prune them back and fertilize them in midsummer after harvest, vigorous determinates produce a light second crop. They are increasingly popular as "double crop" tomatoes in warm climates.

INDETERMINATE TOMATOES: These types of tomatoes produce a summer-long stream of flowers and fruit. The tall, lanky plants require support from stakes, a trellis, or wire cages. Their fruit usually has excellent flavor, and plants remain productive until frost.

GROWING TOMATO SEEDLINGS

You can buy the most popular tomato varieties as bedding plants. Buy them as soon as they arrive in stores, choosing plants that show no signs of flowering or yellowing leaves.

Unless you are ready to plant them within a day or two, transplant the

PEST WATCH
TOMATO HORNWORM

In early summer, colorful green caterpillars with white diagonal stripes on their sides and a fleshy spike or horn on their tails often appear on tomato plants and sometimes on peppers, too. They are tomato hornworms, the larvae of a large moth that hides tiny green eggs on leaf undersides. Growing up to 4 inches long, they eat so many leaves that they seriously weaken plants. Pick them off as soon as you see them. Despite their ferocious appearance and aggressive attitude, tomato hornworms neither sting nor bite.

TOMATO
continued

Like many modern hybrids, 'Celebrity' is resistant to most tomato diseases and can be counted upon for a bountiful crop of round red fruit. It is a vigorous determinate that produces several clusters of fruit in midsummer. If you prune it back and give it adequate water and fertilizer, it will reflower and produce again in fall.

seedlings into 4- or 6-inch pots filled with any good potting soil. Handle the plants by their leaves and roots and avoid touching their fragile stems. Set the plants deep in their new pots, because any section of stem that is buried will grow additional roots. Water well and place the plants under fluorescent lights.

Start unique or unusual varieties from seed about six weeks before your last spring frost date. Tomato seeds germinate best at 75° to 85° F. Grow seedlings under fluorescent lights for 12 hours each day. Adjust the light every few days to keep it 3 inches above the tops of the plants' leaves.

Fertilize seedlings once a week with a half-strength liquid fertilizer. Transplant them to larger pots every three weeks or whenever the plants' roots reach the edges of the containers. Normal room temperature is fine for tomato seedlings, which may grow too fast if temperatures are above 70° F.

TRANSPLANTING TOMATOES

Harden off tomato seedlings for two weeks before transplanting them to the garden. Set plants in the garden after nights are consistently warmer than 50° F. In cool climates, cover the soil with black plastic to help warm it.

Transplant tomatoes on a warm, cloudy day. They need a site with full sun and well-drained soil with a pH between 5.5 and 6.5. Enrich the soil with plenty of organic matter before planting.

Space large indeterminate and vigorous determinate tomatoes at least 24 inches apart. Compact determinates can be grown slightly closer together, but all tomatoes should be spaced far enough apart that air can freely circulate through the foliage when plants are fully grown. Prepare individual planting holes by mixing two shovelfuls of compost into each hole.

Special tomato fertilizers have an analysis of 5-6-5 or 3-5-6, and supply a modest amount of quick-release nitrogen along with phosphorous and potassium. Follow package directions when using these products. Most are applied twice a season—once before

planting and again after the plants have set a number of green fruit the size of a grape.

Plant seedlings deep enough that soil covers at least 2 inches of the main stem. Deep planting protects the stem from wind damage and encourages development of extensive roots.

Protection from cold wind for newly transplanted tomatoes is as important as fertilizer. Cover the transplants with cloches or a plastic tunnel. If you plan to use wire cages to support plants, install them after planting, then wrap the bottom 12 inches of the cages with clear plastic held in place with clothespins. The plastic will buffer strong winds and help keep the seedlings warm.

After the soil warms and the plants begin to grow rapidly, mulch them to help keep soil constantly moist. Tomatoes need a consistent and plentiful supply of water. In many areas, you can wait until after the first fruit have set and the plants have been fertilized to apply an organic mulch. Leave plastic mulch in place all summer. By holding moisture in the soil, it helps to control blossom end rot.

PRUNING AND SUPPORT

Because almost every stem of a determinate tomato will produce flowers and fruit, do not pinch or prune them off. Keep determinate tomatoes upright by surrounding them with

Compact tomatoes such as 'Patio Prize' are ideal for growing in containers in the company of flowers and herbs.

'Brandywine' is considered the taste-test champion among tomatoes, but it needs perfect weather for good fruit set. And people often complain that it has ugly fruit.

circular wire tomato cages or by placing wood stakes between plants and weaving plastic twine between the stakes and plants in a figure-eight design.

Indeterminate tomatoes are so lush and rangy that you should either prune them and tie them to stakes or support them with wire cages. Buy premade cages or make your own from 6-foot lengths of 6-inch-mesh concrete reinforcing wire. In windy areas, stake the cages in place. Attach them to one another at the top to help keep them upright through gusty thunderstorms.

Prune indeterminate plants according to the weather in your climate. Where summers are hot, you may want to leave the plants

unpruned so that leaves shield the fruit from strong sun. In cooler climates, pinching out some of the secondary stems, called suckers, helps open the plants to sunshine, which helps ripen fruit faster.

Cherry tomatoes produce so many small, sweet fruit that one plant may be enough.

HARVEST AND STORAGE

Tomatoes are mature and full-flavored when their color fully develops. However, you can pick fruit as soon as it shows a hint of pink. At this stage, flavor will continue to develop in the fruit whether off or on the vine.

After harvest, keep tomatoes in a warm place until you are ready to eat them. Never chill tomatoes because cool temperatures break down the flavor.

Just before the first fall frost, harvest mature green tomatoes, wrap them loosely in newspaper, and pack them into a box. Kept indoors at room temperature, stored tomatoes will continue to ripen for several weeks.

LOOKING FOR TURNIPS?
See page 77.

SELECTIONS

Choose an assortment of varieties for different purposes. 'Celebrity' (vigorous indeterminate) and 'Better Boy' (indeterminate) are disease-resistant hybrids. In the North, look for early maturing varieties, such as 'Early Girl' (indeterminate). In the South, select heat-resistant cultivars, such as 'Jet Star'.

Yellow or orange tomatoes, such as 'Taxi' (yellow determinate) or 'Husky Gold' (vigorous determinate) offer a change of pace.

Heirloom varieties have interesting shapes. 'Mortgage Lifter' and 'Brandywine' are flavorful, though ugly. Heirloom tomatoes can be temperamental and rarely produce as many tomatoes as disease-resistant hybrids.

Paste tomatoes have solid interiors with little juice. They cook down to a thick sauce. Most plum-shaped paste tomatoes are determinate.

Cherry and currant tomatoes like 'Sungold' and 'Sweet 100' have a sweet, fruity flavor. They are so prolific that you probably will need only one or two plants.

Among indeterminate varieties, 'Big Boy' is a longtime favorite. The first fruit often weigh more than a pound each.

'Enchantment' is a disease-resistant, midseason hybrid with egg-shaped tomatoes. Use it fresh or cooked into sauce.

WATERMELON
Citrullus lanatus

WATERMELON FACTS

Site: Full sun. Well-drained, fertile soil high in organic matter. Consistent, plentiful moisture until fruit begins filling out.

Planting: Sow seed indoors in peat pots, 2–3 weeks before setting out in the garden. Transplant 2 weeks after average last frost. In warm regions, direct sow seed. Plant in hills with three transplants or five to six seeds per hill.

Spacing: Bush types: 3 feet apart each way. Vining types: 3 feet apart in rows 8 feet apart. Thin to three plants per hill.

Care: Mulch. Sturdy trellising is critical in small gardens. As fruit develops, support with netting or fabric.

Harvest: When fruit are full-sized, their surface loses glossy luster, the color on the bottom surface of the fruit changes to a pale yellow, and tendrils on the stems turn dry and brown.

Peculiarities: Anthracnose, wilt, and cucumber beetles. Sensitive to frost. Needs long, warm growing season. To ensure ripening in northern gardens, try growing faster maturing small-fruited cultivars such as 'Garden Baby.'

Start the seeds of seedless watermelons, such as 'Deuce of Hearts', indoors and transplant to the garden after three weeks.

ABOUT WATERMELON

A juicy slice of watermelon is a centuries-old antidote to sweltering summer temperatures. Today, though, you can beat the heat with more than the classic, red-fleshed fruit. Watermelons now also come in yellow and orange, and there are seedless varieties.

Watermelons that grow in the typical large oblong shape require a long, hot growing season. Smaller icebox melons—the ones with fruit weighing 10 pounds or less—ripen in any climate with at least 80 days of warmth.

'Tiger Baby' (below) grows 7- to 10-pound fruit on small, bushy plants. Disease-resistant plants are ideal for small gardens and short seasons.

GROWING WATERMELONS

SITE: Watermelons need full sun and warm, well-drained, slightly acid soil (pH 6.2 to 6.8) that is rich in organic matter. You will need at least five plants to ensure good cross-pollination. Because watermelon vines can grow 10 to 15 feet long, they require a space at least 8 feet wide and 12 feet long for five small icebox melon plants. It takes a plot twice that size to grow large-fruited watermelons.

PLANTING: To get a head start, plant watermelon seeds indoors at about the time of the last spring frost. Sow them in large containers, such as 3-inch peat pots. Thin seedlings to one per pot. Gently break off the sticky seed coats that adhere to the emerging seedlings. If not removed, they can prevent the seedlings' leaves from growing. When the plants are two to three weeks old, transplant them outdoors, disturbing the roots as little as possible.

You must start seedless watermelons indoors, but you can direct sow other varieties into the garden. Plant them in rows or hills spaced 4 feet apart. Before sowing seeds or transplanting seedlings, incorporate a standard application of a balanced fertilizer into the soil. In cool climates, cover prepared soil with sheets of black plastic. Cut holes in the plastic to plant seeds or seedlings.

A month after your last frost, when the soil is warm, sow seeds 1 inch deep and 6 inches apart in rows. If you are using hills, plant four seeds per hill. After the seedlings develop two true leaves, thin the plants to 2 feet apart in rows or to two plants per hill.

WEEDS: Watermelons grow rapidly when nights stay above 60° F. Unless you planted the seedlings in black plastic, thoroughly weed and mulch the open ground between plants as soon as the vines begin to run. Then cover the soil with fabric weed barrier or black plastic. Weeding among established plants mangles the vines, which in turn causes fruit to ripen unevenly.

WATERING: In dry areas, install soaker hoses or a drip irrigation system in your watermelon patch before the vines run. Young plants need about ½ inch of water per week. Later, while the fruit is ripening, the plants' need for water doubles. You can stop irrigating watermelons when the melons are almost ripe—a strategy that may intensify their sweet flavor.

Like cucumbers and squash, watermelons produce both male and female flowers, and only the female flowers can set fruit. Honeybees and other insects help spread the pollen among the flowers. Under good conditions, each plant should set between two and five fruit.

When the plants have set fruit and are producing only a few flowers near the vine tips, fertilize with a balanced, quick-release fertilizer, such as ammonium nitrate. Or apply a soluble liquid fertilizer through a hose-end sprayer to avoid tramping through the vines.

If the season is rainy, carefully place a piece of cardboard or a bed of straw beneath each melon when it is the size of a softball. This will help prevent fruit rot. Other problems you may encounter are anthracnose, a fungal disease, and cucumber beetles, which spread bacterial wilt disease. The best way to avoid these problems is to plant disease-resistant varieties.

For something different, try watermelons with yellow flesh, such as 'Yellow Doll' (above) or 'New Queen', which has orange flesh. Although stores rarely offer them, these watermelons are as sweet and juicy as red-fleshed varieties.

HARVEST AND STORAGE

There are several ways to tell when your watermelons are ripe. With most varieties, the pale spot on the bottom of the melon changes from green or white to creamy yellow. Also, check the curly tendril nearest to the stem of the fruit to see if it is dry and brown. Finally, thump the melon soundly with your finger and listen for a deep thud. Underripe melons will sound high-pitched and tinny.

Leave melons in the garden for a week or so after they ripen or move them into a shady spot outdoors. Unrefrigerated melons will keep for two to three weeks. Storing them in a cool basement will help hold them a little longer.

SELECTIONS

If both space and growing season limit your ability to grow watermelons, choose early-maturing varieties with vines that run only 8 to 10 feet long. 'Yellow Doll', which has yellow flesh, or red-fleshed 'Sugar Baby' are good choices. The vines of 'Tiger Baby' run a little longer, but the delicious striped melons are worth the extra space.

Intermediate-size melons, which weigh between 20 and 30 pounds, usually need 100 days of warm weather to mature. 'Crimson Sweet', along with the heirloom variety called 'Moon and Stars', are classics.

If you want to grow a massive melon, start with the variety called 'Carolina Cross'. As with pumpkins, pick off all but one fruit from each vine. Your mature melon may grow to more than 100 pounds.

Seedless watermelons look like icebox melons on the outside but have very few seeds inside. They produce little pollen, so a few seeds of 'Sugar Baby' or other good pollen producers are included in their seed packets. For this reason, a few melons in a seedless patch will have a normal number of seeds.

As with cantaloupes and other melons, set watermelons on a square of cardboard as they develop to protect them and help them ripen.

THE USDA PLANT HARDINESS ZONE MAP OF NORTH AMERICA

Plants are classified according to the amount of cold weather they can handle. For example, a plant listed as hardy to zone 6 will survive a winter in which the temperature drops to minus 10° F.

Warm weather also influences whether a plant will survive in your region. Although this map does not address heat hardiness, in general, if a range of hardiness zones are listed for a plant, the plant will survive winter in the coldest zone as well as tolerate the heat of the warmest zone.

To use this map, find the approximate location of your community, then match the color band marking that area to the zone key at left.

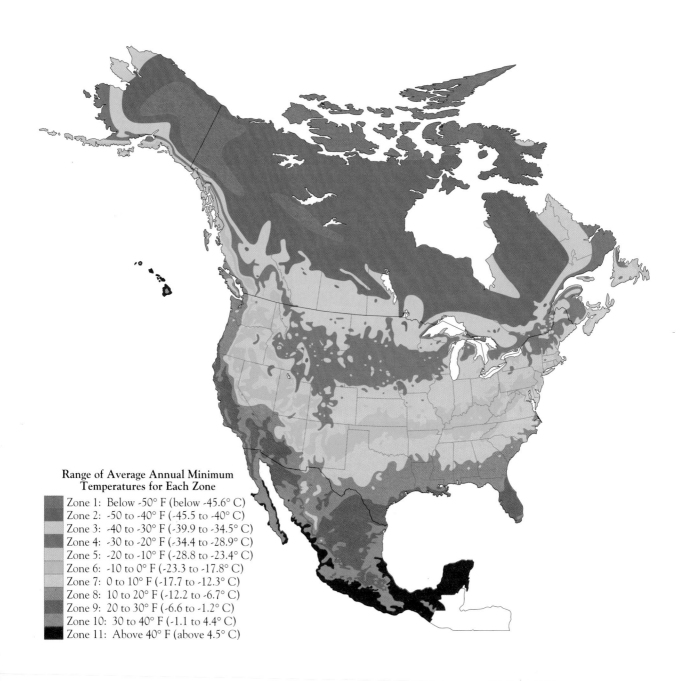

Range of Average Annual Minimum Temperatures for Each Zone

Zone 1: Below -50° F (below -45.6° C)
Zone 2: -50 to -40° F (-45.5 to -40° C)
Zone 3: -40 to -30° F (-39.9 to -34.5° C)
Zone 4: -30 to -20° F (-34.4 to -28.9° C)
Zone 5: -20 to -10° F (-28.8 to -23.4° C)
Zone 6: -10 to 0° F (-23.3 to -17.8° C)
Zone 7: 0 to 10° F (-17.7 to -12.3° C)
Zone 8: 10 to 20° F (-12.2 to -6.7° C)
Zone 9: 20 to 30° F (-6.6 to -1.2° C)
Zone 10: 30 to 40° F (-1.1 to 4.4° C)
Zone 11: Above 40° F (above 4.5° C)

FIRST AND LAST FROST DATES

These maps indicate the average dates for the first and last frosts across North America. Many factors influence the accuracy of these dates. For example, at the bottom of a north-facing hill, spring comes later and fall earlier than on the top of the hill. It wouldn't hurt to contact your local cooperative extension service to find a more precise date for your location.

Light frosts occur when the temperature falls below 33° F. Light frost rarely poses a threat to cool-season vegetables, many of which grow quite well in cold weather in spring and fall.

Warm-season vegetables are a bit more variable. Some quickly succumb to light frost, while others, such as tomatoes, survive until a hard frost (around 28° F) knocks them down. However, it's best to wait until after the last frost in spring to set out warm-season vegetables in the garden and not plan on harvesting much after the first fall frost.

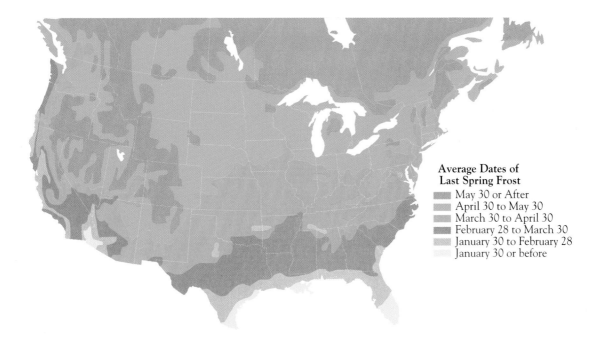

**Average Dates of
Last Spring Frost**
- May 30 or After
- April 30 to May 30
- March 30 to April 30
- February 28 to March 30
- January 30 to February 28
- January 30 or before

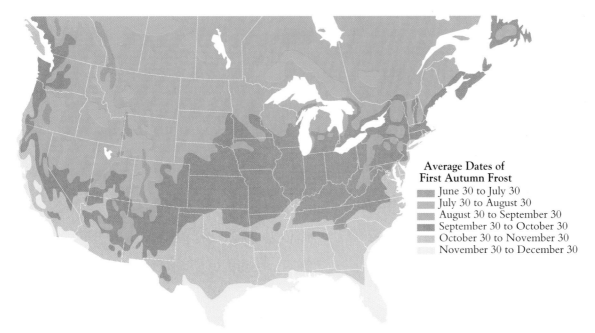

**Average Dates of
First Autumn Frost**
- June 30 to July 30
- July 30 to August 30
- August 30 to September 30
- September 30 to October 30
- October 30 to November 30
- November 30 to December 30

VEGETABLE SOURCES

W. Atlee Burpee & Company
300 Park Avenue
Warminster, PA 18974
800-888-1447
www.burpee.com

The Cook's Garden
PO Box 535
Londonderry, VT 05148
800-457-9703

DeGiorgi Seed Company
6011 'N' Street
Omaha, NE 68117-1634
402-731-3901
800-858-2580

Ferry-Morse Seed Co.
P. O. Box 488
Fulton, KY 42041-0488
800-283-6400 to order
800-283-3400 garden help line
www.ferry-morse.com

Henry Field Seed & Nursery Co.
415 North Burnett
Shenandoah, IA 51602
605-665-9391

The Gourmet Gardener
8650 College Boulevard
Overland Park, KS 66210
913-345-0490
www.gourmetgardener.com

Gurney's Seed & Nursery Co.
110 Capital Street
Yankton, SD 57079
605-665-1930 to order

Harris Seeds
PO Box 22960
60 Saginaw Drive
Rochester, NY 14692-2960
800-514-4441 to order
Fax: 716-442-9386

Johnny's Selected Seeds
Route 1, Box 2580
Foss Hill Road
Albion, ME 04910-9731
207-437-4301 for orders and
    catalog requests
Fax: 800-437-4290
www.johnnyseeds.com

J. W. Jung Seed Co.
335 S. High Street
Randolph, WI 53957-0001
800-297-3123
www.jungseed.com

Mellinger's, Inc.
2310 W. South Range Road
North Lima, OH 44452-9731
330-549-9861
800-321-7444 for orders and
    catalog requests
www.mellingers.com
email: mellgarden@aol.com

Nichols Garden Nursery Inc.
1190 North Pacific Highway NE
Albany, OR 97321-4580
541-928-9280
www.pacificharbor.com/nichols/

Pinetree Garden Seeds
Box 300
616 A Lewiston Road
New Gloucester, ME 04260
207-926-3400
Fax: 888-52SEEDS
www:superseeds.com
email:
    superseeds@worldnet.att.net

Renee's Garden
7389 West Zayante Road
Felton, CA 95018
888-880-7228
Fax: 831-335-7227
www.garden.com/reneesgarden
Call for location of nearest
    nursery.

Shepherd's Garden Seeds
30 Irene Street
Torrington, CT 06790
860-482-3638 for information,
    orders, and catalog
Fax: 860-482-0532
www.shepherdseeds.com

Stokes Seed Inc.
PO Box 548
183 E. Main Street (Fredonia)
Buffalo, NY 14240-0548
716-695-6980
www.stokeseeds.com

Thompson & Morgan
PO Box 1308
220 Farraday Avenue
Jackson, NJ 08527-0308
800-274-7333

Vermont Bean Seed Co.
Garden Lane
Fair Haven, VT 05743
803-663-0217

Territorial Seed Company
PO Box 157
220 Palmer Avenue
Cottage Grove, OR 97424-0061
541-942-9547
www.territorial-seed.com
Regional, national and Canadian
    versions of catalog for year-
    round gardening.

INDEX

Numbers in italics denote photographs or illustrations only. Boldface numbers refer to entries in the "Encyclopedia of Vegetables."

F

Fabric weed barrier, 8
Fall garden activities, 30–31
Families, plant, 7
Fava beans, **40**
Fennel, **55**
    fall, 30
    Florence, 55
Fertilizer, 19–21
    application, *19*, 21
    low nitrogen for cole crops, 42
    container gardens, 15
    ingredients, 19, 20
    parsnips, 76
    pollution, and 21
    seedlings, 25
    tomato, 86
    types, 20–21
    water-soluble and seedlings, 25
Fiber blocks, 24
Field bindweed, 10
Field peas, **69**
Filet beans, **38**
Finocchio, **55**
Fish emulsions, 20
Fishtail weeders, 10
Flea beetles
    arugula, 35
    basil, 37
    Chinese cabbage, 49
    eggplant, 54
    okra, 63
    radishes, 74
Flies, carrot rust, 46
Floating row covers, 11, 26, *29*
Florence fennel, **55**
Frisée, 79
Frost
    dates, first and last, 91
    fall gardening, 30–31
    hardening off, and 25
    hardy vegetables, 31
    pockets, 14
    warm-season vegetables, 23

G

Garden waste, 17
Garlic, 29, **56**
Germination, 27
Grass clippings
    composting, 17
    mulch, 8
    soil amendment, 17
Greenhouse substitutions, 26
Greenhouse seedlings, 25
Gynoecious varieties, 53

H

Hand-weeding, 10
Hardening off, 25

Hardpan, 14, 16
Harvest, timing of, 11, 33. *See also specific crops*
Herbicides, 11
Herbs and pest deterrence, *28*, 29
High-yield vegetables, 6
Hoeing, 10
Honeydews, **60–61**
Horseradish, **57**
Hummingbirds, 39

I

Insecticides, 33
    neem-based, 73
    pollination and, 29
    pyrethrum, 81
    soap, 25
Insects. See also specific crops
    aphids, 29, 49, 63, 71, 77
    asparagus beetles, 36
    beneficial, 29
    butterflies, 66
    cabbage root maggots, 74
    cabbageworm, 42
    carrot rust flies, 46
    Colorado potato beetle, 54
    corn earworm, 50
    cucumber beetles, 52, 60–61
    flea beetles, 35, 37, 49, 54, 63, 74
    indoor seedlings, 25
    leaf miners, 80
    luring beneficial, 29
    managing, 11, 28–29, 32–33
    Mexican bean beetle, 39
    onion root maggots, 65
    rhubarb curculio, 75
    rust flies, carrot, 46
    squash bugs, 61, 81
    squash vine borer, 83
    tarnished plant bugs, 71
    tomato hornworm, 85
Interplanting, 7
Iron deficiency, 19
Irrigation, 9
    drip system, 9
    site selection, 13
    summer, 28

J

Jalapeños, **71**
Jerusalem artichoke, 57, **76**

K

Kale, **45**
    fall, 30
    'Lacinato,' 33
    'Red Russian,' 45
    shade tolerance, 14
Kelp solution, 39
Kitchen, gardening and, 7, 13

Kohlrabi, **45**
    fall, 30
    spring soil, 24

L

Ladybugs, 29
Lamb's lettuce, **78**
Landscape. *See Selecting a Site*, 13-14
Leaf miners, 80
Leeks, 65
    interplanting crops, 7
Lettuce, **58–59**
    'Bibb,' *15*
    'Buttercrunch,' 58
    fall soil, 30
    interplanting crops, 7
    'Rosalita,' 59
    'Ruby Ball,' *15*
    shade tolerance, 14
    spring soil, 24
    'Sierra,' 58
Light and indoor seedlings, 25
Lima beans, **40**
Lime, 17, 19
Loam, 16
Low spots and site selection, 14

M

Mâche, **78**
Magnesium, 19
Manure, 8, 18
    potatoes and, 72
Marigolds, *28*, 29
Maturation times, 33
Melons, **60–61**
Mesclun, 24, 30, **78**
    fall, 30
    spring, 24
Mexican bean beetle, 39
Micronutrients, 19
Microorganisms and fertilizers, 20
Milk-carton cloche, 26
Moisture, soil, 16–17
    mulch, 8
    watering requirements, 9
    weeding and, 10
Mosaic virus, cucumber, 53
Mulch, 8, 10. *See also specific crops*
    fall application, 31
    paths, 8
    summer application, 28
    watering requirements, 9
Muskmelons, **60–61**
Mustard, **62**
    fall, 30
    'Tatsoi,' 62
    spring, 24

N

Napa Chinese cabbage, **49**
Natural organic material, 20
Nematodes, 46

Newspaper mulch, 8
Nitrogen, 19
  deficiency, 19
  fertilizers, 20–21
  manure, 18
  sawdust mulch, 8
  spinach, 80
Nitrogen fixation
  bacterial innoculant, 68
  beans, 38
  cover crops, 18
  peas, 68–69
No-chill seedlings, 24
Notebook, keeping garden, 5, 11
Nutrient ratio, 21
Nutrients, 19-21
Nutritional deficiency, 19

O
Okra, 14, **63**
Onion root maggots, 65
Onions, **64–65**
  pest deterrence, 28, 29
  start indoors, 24
Organic matter, adding, 17–18

P
Parsley, 24, **66**
Parsnips, **76–77**
  cold hardiness, *31*
  spring soil, 24
Parthenocarpic varieties, 53
Paths, mulched, 8
Peanuts, **67**
Peas, **68–69**
  field, 69
  garden, 68–69
  spring soil, 24
  'Mississippi Silver,' 69
  'Pinkeye Purple Hull,' 69
Peat pellets and pots, 24
Peppers, **70–71**
  cloches and, 26
  container gardens, 15
  'Gypsy,' 70
  nitrogen requirement, 19
  start indoors, 24
Pests, managing, 8, 28–29, 32–33. See
  also Insects; *specific pests*
PH, soil, 17, 19
Phosphorus, 19
Pinto beans, 39
Planning, 5
  arrangement, 14–15
  fall cleanup and, 31
  movement within garden, 15
  recordkeeping, 5, 11
  rotation of crops, 7
  seasonal succession, 6
  site selection, *12–13*, 13–14
  size of garden, 7
  soil preparation, 16–18
Plant families, 7

Planting. *See also* Transplanting
  seedlings; *specific crops*
  interplanting crops, 7
  schedule, 5
  spring, 24, 27
Plastic mulch, 8, 11
Plastic tunnels, 26
Pole beans, **39**
Pollination, 29
  corn, 29, 51
  melons, 60–61
  squash, 82
Potassium, 19
Potatoes, **72–73**
  spring soil, 24
Potato scab, 72
Powdery mildew
  cucumbers, 52–53
  peas, 69
Priming Seeds, 51
Pumpkins, 81, **83**
Pyrethrum, 81

Q
Quick-release fertilizers, 21. *See also*
  Using Fertilizers, 19-21
Quackgrass, *10*

R
Raddicchio, **79**
Radishes, **74**
  fall, 30
  interplanting crops, 7
  spring, 24
Raised beds, 14–15
  drainage, 14
Rashes, 63
Recordkeeping, 5, 11
Recycled containers, seedlings, 24
Reference materials, storing, 5
Rhubarb, 24, **75**
Rhubarb curculio, 75
Romaine lettuce, 59
Root crops, 76–77
Root growth, seedlings, 25
Root-knot nematode, 63
Root zone watering, 9
Rotation, crop, 7, 32
Row covers, 11, 26, *29*, 32
Rows, planting in, 14
Runner beans, **39**
Rutabaga, **77**
Ryegrass, 18

S
Salad greens, **78–79**
  chicory, 79
  container gardens, 15
  endive, 79
  mâche, 78
  mesclun, 78
Sandy soil, 9, 16

Sawdust
  mulch, 8
  soil amendment, 17
Scallions, **65**
  fall garden, 30
Scarlet runner beans, 39
Seasons, gardening, 6, 22–31
  day length, 22
  extending-devices, 26
  fall, 30–31
  matching crops, 23
  spring, 27
  summer, 28–29
  winter, 24–25
Seeds
  planting, 27
  soaking, 27
  starting indoors, 24–25, 86
  See also Transplanting seedlings
Seedlings, 24
Shade-tolerant vegetables, 14
Shading plants, 14, 28–29
Shallots, 64–65
Shell beans, 38, 39
Side-dressing, 19, 21
Site selection, *12–13*, 13–14. *See also*
  specific crops
Size of garden, 7, 15
Slugs, 8, 28, 37
Snap beans, 38–39
Snow peas, 68, 69
Soaker hoses, 9
Soil, 16–18
  amendments, 17–18
  hardpan, 14, 16
  indoor seedlings, 24
  testing, 17, 19
  type, 9, 16–17
Soilless mix, 24
Solanine, 72–73
Solarization, 11
Sowing seeds, 24, 27
Spacing, 14, 32. *See also specific crops*
Spinach, **80**
  bolting, 24
  day length and, 22
  fall, 30
  nitrogen requirement, 19
  shade tolerance, 14
  spring, 24
  'Space,' 80
Spotted cucumber beetle, 60, 61
Spring planting, 24, 27
Sprouting, seedlings, 25
Spurge, 10
Squash, **81–83**
  container gardens, 15
  garden arrangement, 14
  pollinating, 82
  summer squash, 81–82
  winter squash, 82–83
Squash bugs, 61, 81
Squash vine borer, 83

METRIC CONVERSIONS

U.S. Units to Metric Equivalents			Metric Units to U.S. Equivalents		
To Convert From	Multiply By	To Get	To Convert From	Multiply By	To Get
Inches	25.4	Millimeters	Millimeters	0.0394	Inches
Inches	2.54	Centimeters	Centimeters	0.3937	Inches
Feet	30.48	Centimeters	Centimeters	0.0328	Feet
Feet	0.3048	Meters	Meters	3.2808	Feet
Yards	0.9144	Meters	Meters	1.0936	Yards
Square inches	6.4516	Square centimeters	Square centimeters	0.1550	Square inches
Square feet	0.0929	Square meters	Square meters	10.764	Square feet
Square yards	0.8361	Square meters	Square meters	1.1960	Square yards
Acres	0.4047	Hectares	Hectares	2.4711	Acres
Cubic inches	16.387	Cubic centimeters	Cubic centimeters	0.0610	Cubic inches
Cubic feet	0.0283	Cubic meters	Cubic meters	35.315	Cubic feet
Cubic feet	28.316	Liters	Liters	0.0353	Cubic feet
Cubic yards	0.7646	Cubic meters	Cubic meters	1.308	Cubic yards
Cubic yards	764.55	Liters	Liters	0.0013	Cubic yards

To convert from degrees Fahrenheit (F) to degrees Celsius (C), first subtract 32, then multiply by 5/9.

To convert from degrees Celsius to degrees Fahrenheit, multiply by 9/5, then add 32.